CAMPAIGN 304

DARWIN 1942

The Japanese attack on Australia

BOB ALFORD

ILLUSTRATED BY JIM LAURIER

Series editor Marcus Cowper

First published in Great Britain in 2017 by Osprey Publishing,
PO Box 883, Oxford, OX1 9PL, UK
1385 Broadway, 5th Floor, New York, NY 10018, USA
E-mail: info@ospreypublishing.com

Osprey Publishing, part of Bloomsbury Publishing Plc
OSPREY is a trademark of Osprey Publishing, a division of Bloomsbury
Publishing Plc.
A CIP catalogue record for this book is available from the British Library.

Print ISBN: 9781472816870
PDF e-book ISBN: 9781472816887
ePub e-book ISBN: 9781472816894

Index by Fionbar Lyons
Typeset in Sabon and Myraid Pro
Battlescene artwork by Jim Laurier
Maps by Bounford.com
3D BEVs by The Black Spot
Originated by PDQ Media, Bungay, UK
Printed in Hong Kong through Worldprint Ltd.

17 18 19 20 21 10 9 8 7 6 5 4 3 2

Osprey Publishing supports the Woodland Trust, the UK's leading woodland
conservation charity. Between 2014 and 2018 our donations are being
spent on their Centenary Woods project in the UK.

www.ospreypublishing.com
To find out more about our authors and books visit **www.
ospreypublishing.com**. Here you will find extracts, author interviews,
details of forthcoming events and the option to sign up for our newsletter.

AUTHOR'S NOTE

Just 74 days after the attacks on Pearl Harbor by Japanese carrier-borne
aircraft and following weeks of rapid victories, the Japanese Navy launched
188 aircraft from four of those same carriers and carried out a devastating
morning attack on the port, township and airfields of Darwin in Australia's
far north. A further attack against the air force station was carried out by 54
land-based bombers in a noon raid.

These attacks of February 19, 1942 have been well documented over the
years. Douglas Lockwood's enduring *Australia's Pearl Harbour* (sic), more
recently re-released as *Australia Under Attack*, is devoted exclusively to the
day's events in an eyewitness account as he was present in Darwin at the
time. His work has formed the basis for most accounts of the raids.

The account by Australian naval officer Owen Griffiths in his *Darwin Drama*
also relates an eyewitness account before addressing other events, while
Alan Powell's encyclopaedic work, *The Shadow's Edge*, provides an excellent
background to and details of the raids and is the only publication dealing
with all aspects of Australia's northern war.

Other works, including Bill Bartsch's *Every Day a Nightmare*, Robert Rayner's
The Army and the Defence of Darwin Fortress and James Rorrison's *Nor the Years
Contemn*, all go into detail and are excellent references. All address the initial
raids across the board and all relate to broader periods of time and events.
This account deliberately avoids going into detail about the attacks on
shipping, the township, wharf and other installations other than in a very
broad sense and from the perspective of the Japanese participants where
that information is available. Instead it focuses upon the aerial activities,
though even they are the tip of the iceberg of what took place.

With more information and particularly material from the Japanese archives
becoming available as each day passes, the fading memories of those who
were in Darwin that day and the families of those veterans, no doubt much
more will emerge to fill the gaps in the material currently available and
expand both our knowledge and the historical record accordingly.

ACKNOWLEDGMENTS.

The author wishes to express his sincere thanks to the following individuals
for their invaluable assistance in the preparation of this work and to those
veterans and individuals whose names appear as the donors of photographs:
In Australia: Stephen Ashford, Craig Bellamy, Gordon Birkett, Pauleen Cass,
Norm Cramp, Liam Carroll at Darwin City Council, Stuart Duncan, Rick
Hanning, John Haslett, Peter Ingman, Shane Johnston, Des Lambert, Dr.
Tom Lewis, Bob Livingstone, Bob and Misako Piper, Prof. Alan Powell, Tony
Simons, Owen Veal and David Vincent.
In the USA: David Aiken, William Bartsch, Jeff Donahoo, Margaret Glover,
Don Kehn Jr., Ed de Kiep, Matthew Jones, James F. Lansdale, Jim Long,
Robert F. McMahon, Andrew Obluski, Edward Rogers, Osamu Tagaya, Ron
Werneth and James Zobel.
In Japan: Ikuhiko Hata, Ryusuke Ichiguru and Dr. Yasuho Izawa.
In the United Kingdom: Marcus Cowper of Ilios Publishing for his guidance
and Nick Millman.

EXPLANATORY NOTES

While codenames for Japanese aircraft were not introduced until late 1942,
Japanese aircraft types are described initially as manufacturer, type and
codename in acknowledging the reader's familiarity with them.
Accordingly, they are described initially as Aichi D3A1 Val, then as D3A1 Val
and henceforth as Val, Mitsubishi A6M2 Zeke, A6M2 Zeke, Zeke and so on.
Times are given as either Japan time or Darwin time. In some cases they are
qualified to reconcile the differences in times provided by Allied and
Japanese records. On January 1, 1942, Darwin time was brought forward by
one hour for Daylight Saving Time, making the time difference 90 minutes
instead of the normal 30 minutes. Thus a Japan time quoted as 0622 in the
case of the first takeoff from the carriers on February 19, 1942 is 0752
Darwin time. Clocks were readjusted on March 29, 1942.
Japanese names used throughout are, unless noted otherwise, presented in
the western style, that is, with the given name followed by the family name.
Unless where otherwise noted the Japanese terms for naval flying units
and ranks are used in lieu of the Allied equivalents, which often varied in
their designations between services.
While some photos are not of high quality they are of significance in their
content and in being scanned from original wartime images.
Unless annotated otherwise, photos are from the author's collection.
The original donors of wartime and other images are acknowledged in
the captions.

CONTENTS

The extent of Japanese expansion through Asia, post February 19, 1942

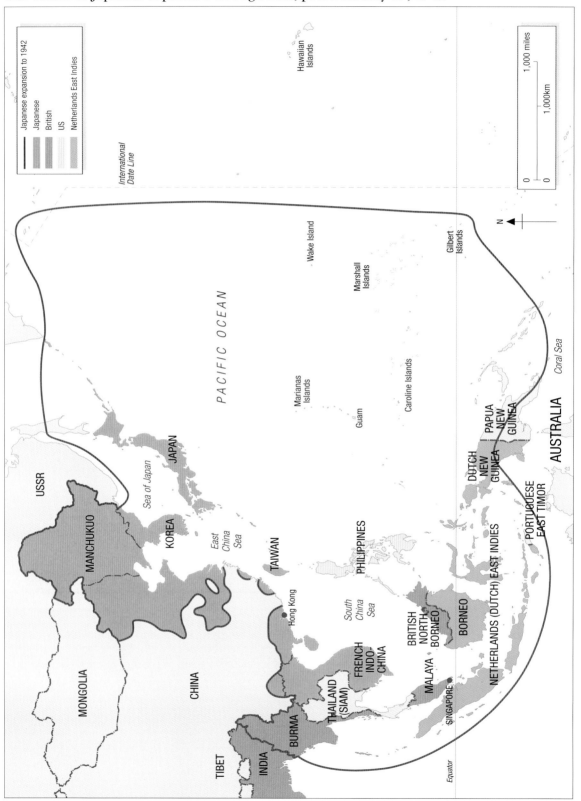

ORIGINS AND BACKGROUND

A THREAT EVOLVES

From as early as 1917 the resource-rich Netherlands East Indies (NEI – now Indonesia) was in the sights of the Japanese as they looked towards their nation's future. Yasaburo Takekoshi, Japanese historian, politician and advocate of Japanese expansion, wrote of the need for Japan to continue the exploitation of China's resources, but also to devote its power to acquiring the NEI and extending its colonies southward. Printed in the *New York Times* of April 22, 1917, Takekoshi's article should have sounded a warning to the Western nations. However Japan was an ally during World War I and the suggestion was seemingly waved aside. Takekoshi also broached the subject of the food staple, rice: "It is therefore necessary for Japan to look to such places as Java and Sumatra as sources of rice supply… she has to look to the islands of the South Pacific for supplies of rubber." Oil was not mentioned but it was no doubt implicit.

Japan had long been in the minds of Australians as the nation they most feared. The American entry to the Philippines in 1892 was seen as the beginnings of a possible British–American alliance against the Japanese. However, it failed to materialize and the defeat of the Russian fleet by the

On August 20, 1908, the US Navy's "Great White Fleet" arrived in Sydney during its circumnavigation of the globe, in part to demonstrate American naval power following Japan's 1905 defeat of the Russian fleet. A range of souvenir programs, postcards and memorabilia marked the enthusiastic welcome of the fleet to Australia.

Japanese in 1905, coinciding with the withdrawal of the Royal Navy from the Pacific, raised alarm in Australia. "We have been living in a fool's paradise," Alan McLean, a former deputy prime minister, warned, "We now find one of the great naval and military powers within a very short distance of our shores."

The Minister for Defence, George Pearce, went further, warning: "Japan has shown that she is an aggressive nation ... that she is desirous of pushing out all round... Is there any other nation that offers such a temptation to Japan as Australia does?" The University of Sydney Chancellor and President of the National Defence League, Sir Normand MacLaurin, echoed the anti-Japanese sentiment, stating, "Japan is the possible, if not probable, enemy of the future."

A visit to Australia by President Theodore Roosevelt's "Great White Fleet" in September 1908 saw pro-American and anti-Japanese sentiments continue when the premier of New South Wales, G.C. Wade, stated that Australia looked to America "as her natural ally in the coming struggle against Japanese domination," no doubt in the shadow of the Japanese destruction of the Russian fleet three years earlier.

In the event, Japan was an ally during World War I. Indeed the heavy cruiser *Ibuki* was involved in the chase of the German cruiser *Emden*, though it was assigned to protect the Australian cruiser *Sydney*'s flank as *Emden* was sunk off the Western Australian coast. As part of its spoils of war, Japan gained control over German mandates in the Pacific despite Australia's objections to its "deeply rooted mistrust of Japan, and [our] emphatic protest on behalf of the Commonwealth against Japan's right or even claim to the Marshalls, Carolines, and Ladrones [Marianas]," wrote Prime Minister Billy Hughes. The British Prime Minister, Lloyd George, reminded Hughes of the pledge made to Japan that its claims would be supported and with the stroke of a pen a huge swathe of the Pacific basin extended Japan's reach towards Australia and the NEI. Despite this, however, the territorial gains failed to increase the raw materials, including oil, tin and rubber, or the food to support the growth of Japanese industries and population.

Darwin welcomed a number of visiting Japanese naval training ships during the 1930s, including these officers from *Kaiwo Maru*, who visited Darwin from June 23–25, 1936. Captain Myamoto and his officers were afforded an official welcome and dinner during their visit. (Charles Micet Collection NT Library)

In 1936 the Australian Chief of General Staff, Maj. Gen. John Lavarack, inspected Darwin's defences and those of its hinterland. Among his conclusions were that, despite a number of natural barriers, mostly mangroves, "no obstacles exist anywhere that would make an approach to Port Darwin by an enemy land force impossible." He also warned of the potential of the Japanese pearling fleet to cause problems in defence: "each carries a crew of from 10 to 12 Japanese [and] … some of them carry qualified navigators … it is certain that a considerable portion, if not most, of the Japanese have had either Naval or Military training. The crews could, of course, be increased and military stores provided without our knowledge." The Japanese pearling fleets had posed problems across the north coast for some time and, despite the best efforts of the authorities, including those of Capt. C.T.G. Haultain and the patrol vessel *Larrakia* in fishery and security patrols, the illegal activities of Japanese vessels continued. Three vessels were caught inside territorial waters off an Aboriginal reserve in 1937 and after shots were fired they were arrested and taken to Darwin. Following a controversial and protracted court case the Japanese won and in part it was hailed as "the opening salvo of the Pacific War."

On May 1, 1938 the *New York Times* ran an article by Hugh Byas under the headline: JAPAN BUILDS A NAVY FOR AN EXPANDING EMPIRE; Control of Distant Seas Is Sought To Assure Japan's Industrial Might. Citing Takekoshi, the article stated, "It is as clear as daylight, that Java and Sumatra will form a very convenient base for Japan's foes, whoever these foes [might be]." By the late 1930s the NEI was described as one of the richest colonies in the world, mainly because of the vast oil reserves, while rubber, tin, rice and spices added to the attraction.

Japan continued her expansionist policies southward – even while engaged in wars in Manchuria from September 1931 and China from July 1937 – all the while continuing with the development of an already formidable military. At the same time the Japanese saw America as reneging on its role as a dependable supplier of oil and, with America's opposition to Japan's expansionist policies, Japan was isolated by a trade embargo, including oil, imposed by Britain, America, Australia, the Dutch and China in July 1941. On November 26 the American Secretary of State, Cordell Hull, demanded the withdrawal of Japanese forces from China and Indo-China (Vietnam) in accordance with a Nine-Power Treaty of the 1920s. However the Japanese had decided on war in September and for them there was no turning back.

The Japanese considered themselves to be in an intolerable position and, with their leaders painting the country as the victim, enthusiasm for war only grew. In October 1941 Lt.Gen. Hideki Tojo and his military government replaced the Japanese Prime Minister, Prince Fumimaro Konoye, and a subsequent statement by Japan clearly indicated that it considered East Asia and the South Seas as its interest alone. Japan continued its expansionist policies and prepared for war.

On November 30, 1941, the British Prime Minister, Winston Churchill, urged Roosevelt to inform Japan, "any further aggressions would compel you to place the gravest issues before Congress, or words to that effect." He called Roosevelt again on December 6, urging the President, with the assistance of Australia's Ambassador, Richard Casey, and others, to appeal to the Emperor Showa, Hirohito, on a personal level. If no reply was forthcoming within 48 hours, Japan should then be "warned" against further aggression. It was too late.

JAPAN ATTACKS

The Japanese struck the following day, December 7 (American time) at Pearl Harbor and at points throughout the Pacific including the Philippines, Guam, Wake Island, Hong Kong, Kota Bahru in northern Malaya and Singora (Songkhla) in southern Thailand – the last two across the International Dateline some hours ahead of the Pearl Harbor strikes, on December 8. These events have been well documented and need no retelling here.

On December 8 Curtin informed Australians that the nation was at war with Japan and two days later the "unsinkable" Royal Navy battleships *Prince of Wales* and *Repulse* were sunk off Malaya by Japanese bombers. The Royal Navy had been bombed out of the Far East and Australia was effectively on her own.

Singapore's ability to provide any viable defence in the face of a concerted attack was also seriously under doubt, as Australia had stressed on a number of occasions. Churchill had cut back defences in the Far East, all the while maintaining that a military build-up would continue and that three months' notice would be provided of any Japanese aggression. Churchill's duplicity did not end there. His priority was Europe and, unknown to Australia, he had entered into an agreement with President Roosevelt to allocate men and *matériel* to that theatre. Firstly however, he needed America's involvement in the war.

Australia's Foreign Minister, Herbert "Doc" Evatt, had predicted Churchill's agenda as early as November 22, 1941, when he confided to Australia's recently appointed Prime Minister, John Curtin, the "United Kingdom is willing to run the risk [of war with the Japanese] for the 'good prospect' of active American participation." Evatt's words were prophetic. As America entered the war on December 7 Churchill was elated, commenting that he was extremely content following the Pearl Harbor raids as America was now firmly involved and on Britain's side. Curtin was not so elated, though probably relieved that after having feigned neutrality for two years America was now an active participant in the Pacific conflict. Curtin

An aerial view of the initial attack on US Naval ships and facilities at Pearl Harbour, December 7, 1941. While the Japanese sank or damaged many vessels and destroyed shore facilities and aircraft, they missed the greatest prize, the American carriers.

海軍省賛下　マレー沖海戦　朝日新聞社主催大東亜戦争美術展覧會　中村研一筆

The Japanese propagandists made the most of the sinking of the British capital ships *Prince of Wales* and *Repulse*. Kenichi Nakamura depicted the scene in his painting "The Battle of the Malayan Sea," which was also produced as a postcard.

demanded that Churchill now live up to Britain's agreement to provide for Australia's defence. However, Churchill maintained that a Japanese invasion of Australia was inconceivable and instead traveled to Washington to concentrate Roosevelt's mind fully on Europe.

Understandably Curtin's government was far from happy with the Churchill–Roosevelt agreement, particularly in view of the rapid advances being made by the Japanese and what was seen as a very real threat to Australia. The one beacon of hope for American involvement, it seemed, was that of Maj. Gen. Dwight D. Eisenhower. A week after Pearl Harbor he reported in response to a directive by the Chief of Staff, Gen. George C. Marshall, "our base must be Australia, and we must start at once to expand it and secure our communications to it. In the last we dare not fail."

THE RISE AND FALL OF ABDACOM

An important part of any moves to make Australia, and northern Australia in particular, a base for the Americans in the Pacific was the containment of the Japanese moves south and the defence of the so-called "Malay Barrier" with Java and Timor the southernmost points of the vast archipelago of the NEI.

The process had commenced informally during 1941, when the Americans belatedly began to ferry Boeing B-17 Fortresses across the Pacific after earlier dismissing the need for bombers or the establishment of bases there. Following Gen. Douglas MacArthur's belief that the Philippines could be defended, the decision was urgently reviewed and the search for air routes to the Philippines, while avoiding the Japanese-held islands, began.

In August 1941 two US Navy Catalina flying boats flew a group from Honolulu to investigate possible bomber staging airfields at Rabaul, Port Moresby and Darwin. With Port Moresby and Darwin recommended, B-17s began flying staging flights over the Pacific with the first, nine B-17s of the 14th Provisional Squadron, Hawaiian Air Force, arriving at Darwin from Port Moresby on September 10. They flew on to Manila two days later and 17 more from the 19th Bombardment Group made the trip during the next few weeks. The Americans were making up for lost time.

In early November MacArthur appointed Maj. Gen. Lewis H. Brereton as Commander Far East Air Force (FEAF) and on November 6 ordered him to proceed to Australia. There he was to survey the trans-Pacific air ferry route from Australia to the Philippines and Java, and assess an extension to Singapore and China. In a farsighted move by MacArthur, Brereton was also instructed to prepare bases in northern Australia and the Malay Barrier, through which the USAAF could operate. "Never at any time did he fail to realise that, if a campaign in the Philippines was unsuccessful," Brereton wrote, "it would be essential … to provide adequate defense of Northern Australia, the Dutch East Indies, and the Malay Peninsula."

It was only a matter of time before MacArthur's prediction was realized, though it was not the fall of the Philippines that was the catalyst. With the Japanese taking all before them, the defense of the "Malay Barrier" and, in turn it can be argued, Australia's defense and its perceived role as an Allied base, became the priority. Darwin's potential for expansion was quickly realized, but only if the "Malay Barrier" could be held and that was a difficult if not impossible task.

As a result ABDACOM, the American–British–Dutch–Australian Command, was formed on January 3, 1942 to provide for the joint defence of the barrier drawn from Burma and Malaya through Singapore to Borneo and the archipelago now known as Indonesia. It was a huge area and a huge responsibility for those appointed to its defence.

That responsibility fell upon the British general, Sir Archibald Wavell, as Supreme Commander and representatives of the various countries involved. Wavell was to "receive his orders from an appropriate joint body who will be responsible to me as the Minister of Defence and to the President of the United States who is also Commander-in-Chief of all United States forces," Churchill wrote.

Wavell arrived in Singapore on January 7, 1942 and on the 18th he moved his headquarters to Lembang near Bandoeng on Java. He must have wondered what he had walked into, commenting that he had heard of being left "holding the baby" but ABDACOM was more like twins. His command was complex, the area he was expected to control was huge, his available forces were spread very thin and the difficulty in coordinating four nationalities and their own military and political agendas made for a formidable challenge.

CHRONOLOGY

Thursday February 19, 1942

0752hrs — 188 aircraft begin taking off from four Japanese aircraft carriers 220 miles from Darwin in the Timor Sea, the last taking off at 0845hrs. The strike force, comprising 81 B5N2 Kate level bombers, 71 D3A1 Val dive-bombers, and 36 A6M2 Zeke escort fighters, sets course for Darwin.

0800hrs — Two US Navy Catalina flying boats take off from Darwin on patrol. One is flown by Lt. Thomas Moorer and his crew.

0915hrs — Lieutenant Moorer sights the Filipino freighter and blockade runner, *Florence D*. Japanese aircraft sight his Catalina shortly afterwards. Nine Zekes from the carrier *Kaga* are detached and one (PO1c Yoshikazu Nagahama) shoots it down. The crew survives and is picked up by the *Florence D*.

0915hrs — Ten US P-40 fighters take off for Timor and on to Java but are advised to return to Darwin on learning of deteriorating weather over Timor.

0935hrs — A warning of a large force of unidentified aircraft is sent by Father McGrath at Bathurst Island Mission to the VID coastal radio station in Darwin. It is logged and relayed to RAAF Darwin and other headquarters at 0937hrs but the aircraft are suggested to be the US P-40 fighters returning to Darwin.

0940hrs — The main Japanese force crosses the coast east of Darwin and then turns over the 22-Mile peg – the distance from the Darwin Post Office – on its approach to the town from the southeast. The eight Zeke fighters from *Kaga* track straight for Darwin, leaving Nagahama to follow.

0940hrs — The returning P-40 fighters begin landing at the RAAF Station, leaving five to patrol over Darwin.

0937–0945hrs — Two of the patrolling P-40s are shot down and another pilot badly wounded in initial combat by PO1c Yoshikazu Nagahama from *Kaga*. The dogfights are witnessed and reported by 2/14 Field Regiment and 19 Machine Gun Regiment personnel.

0950hrs — 2 Heavy Anti-Aircraft Battery at Coonawarra engages approaching enemy aircraft with 60 rounds from 3.7-inch guns. 14 HAA Battery also reports sighting and engaging enemy aircraft at 15,000 feet.

0957hrs — The remaining eight *Kaga* Zekes pass over the boom net and attack the minesweeper HMAS *Gunbar*.

0958hrs — The Kate high-level bombers arrive over Darwin and release their ordnance. Each carries one 800kg bomb.

0958hrs — The town's 18 antiaircraft guns at the town Oval, Fannie Bay, McMillans, Coonawarra and Elliott Point open fire on the enemy aircraft.

0959hrs — The wharf and shipping are struck by 800kg bombs, with 23 "wharfies" killed. The air raid siren sounds.

0959hrs — Kate high-level bombers hit the town; the post office is the largest of several buildings hit; six women and three men on its staff die, along with the postmaster. Over 10, 000 people, mainly military, are in Darwin, with most civilians evacuated beforehand leaving only 63 women and a civilian population of some 2,000.

1002hrs	The remaining P-40 fighters attempt to take off and intercept the enemy aircraft. All are downed, with the squadron commander, Maj. Floyd Pell, and three other pilots killed in both combats.
1003hrs	As the Kate high-level bombers complete their bombing run, Val dive-bombers attack shipping, the Parap Civil 'Drome and the RAAF Station, while Zekes strafe targets of opportunity. Each Val carries one 250kg bomb.
1010hrs	Six ships are sunk in the harbour, with the biggest concentrated loss of life aboard the destroyer, USS *Peary*. Bombed and on fire, *Peary* sinks with the loss of 88 of its ship's company, though witnesses attest it fought to the last. Two more ships are damaged enough that they sink over the next few days.
1015hrs	One Val dive-bomber attacking the RAAF Station is hit by ground fire and crashes at Ironstone Ridge east of Darwin, killing both crew members who are buried nearby.
1025–1028hrs	*Neptuna* and her load of depth charges and ammunition blow up at the main wharf with an explosion resembling a mushroom cloud. Large pieces of superstructure are scattered over the area and town.
1028hrs	The Qantas flying boat G-AEUB, *Camilla*, takes off; shortly after the freighter *Neptuna* blows up.
1030hrs	The strike force commander, Mitsuo Fuchida, signals the last of the enemy aircraft to return to the carrier task force. Aerial photos are taken of the harbour and damage to the town.
1035hrs	One Zeke damaged by ground fire force lands on Melville Island where the pilot, PO1c Hajime Toyoshima from the carrier *Hiryu*, is later captured. He is

the first Japanese prisoner of war to be taken in Australia.

1040hrs	"All clear" sounded over Darwin.
1045hrs	Nine Zekes from the carrier *Soryu* attack the Filipino freighter, *Don Isidro*, off Bathurst Island during their return to the carrier task force.
1158hrs	A second raid by 54 Betty and Nell land-based bombers flying from Kendari and Ambon begins. They attack the RAAF station with 531 bombs causing extensive damage. Both raids result in at least 236 deaths and a further 300 wounded. Much of the town's infrastructure is destroyed or damaged, six ships are sunk and 27 Allied aircraft destroyed.
1210hrs	One damaged Zeke from the carrier *Kaga* ditches near the task force and its pilot is picked up by a destroyer from the carrier task force. A Kate from *Kaga* is also thought to have ditched and its crew to have been rescued.
1215hrs	One damaged Val dive-bomber from the carrier *Soryu* ditches and its crew members are picked up by a destroyer from the carrier task force.
1317hrs	"All clear" sounded.
1626–1642hrs	The US-employed Filipino freighter, *Don Isidro*, is attacked off Bathurst Island by Val dive-bombers from carrier *Soryu*. *Don Isidro* catches fire and eventually ends up beached off Bathurst Island. At the same time the *Florence D* is attacked and sunk north of Bathurst Island by Val dive-bombers from *Hiryu*.
	The survivors from both vessels land at different locations on Bathurst Island and are returned to Darwin by HMAS *Warrnambool* on February 20 and 21, 1942.

OPPOSING COMMANDERS

THE ALLIES

General Sir Archibald Wavell was a career soldier. He had served in World War I and, in World War II, he was initially in the Middle East as Commander-in-Chief. He led the British and Commonwealth forces to victory against the Italians in December 1940, only to face defeat by the Germans in the Western Desert in April 1941. He was appointed Commander-in-Chief India in July 1941 and following agreement at the Arcadia Conference he was appointed Supreme Commander to ABDACOM on December 29, 1941.

Wavell's first challenge was to form a cohesive command and in this he was fortunate to have the services of **Lt. Gen. George H. Brett** USAAF as his deputy commander and **Lt. Gen. Henry R. Pownall**, the former Commander-in-Chief of the British Far East Command in South East Asia. **Lt. Gen. Hein Ter Poorten**, Royal Netherlands East Indies Army, was the commander of land forces and was in direct command of the NEI land forces, while **Maj. Gen. Ian Playfair**, British Army, was his deputy and chief of staff, land forces.

General Sir Archibald Wavell faced a huge challenge in commanding ABDACOM. Here he meets with Adm. Hart (left), the Dutch Governor General's representative Lt. Col. Lanzing (third left) and Lt. Gen. Brett (right). (AWM, Negative 011603)

The air forces came under the RAF's **Air Marshal Sir Richard Peirse** with **Maj. Gen. Lewis H. Brereton** USAAF as deputy commander. **Adm. Thomas C. Hart**, US Navy, was made Commander, Naval Forces and remained until February 12, 1942 when **Adm. Conrad Helfrich**, Royal Netherlands Navy, took over. A mix of Americans and British filled the majority of the positions while the Dutch and Australians, both experienced in Japanese tactics, were assigned to what amounted to little more than advisory roles.

While Wavell was overall Supreme Commander of ABDACOM, Darwin was in effect a staging point for the American pursuit (fighter) squadrons flying through to Java. In Darwin there was a realization that with the fighting only two hours away an attack by the Japanese was only a matter of time.

In charge of Darwin's defenses was **Maj. Gen. David V.J. Blake**. Commissioned in the Australian Army in 1916 he became the first commander of No. 3 Squadron Australian Flying Corps and was responsible for arranging the burial of Manfred von Richthofen. In September 1941 he was appointed Officer Commanding 7th Military District encompassing the Northern Territory in Darwin and incorporated into ABDACOM. Blake was present during the February 19 attacks, following which he withdrew his forces from Darwin in expectation of a land attack. His action, deemed a tactical error, saw him moved to command the Lines of Communication NT area later that year.

Blake was supported by the Air Force and Navy in **Group Captain Frederick R.W. Scherger RAAF** and **Captain Edward P. Thomas**. Scherger was a graduate of the Duntroon Military College before transferring to the Air Force in 1925. He became one of Australia's top airmen, earning an AFC in 1940. Promoted to group captain, he was acting commander of the North Western Area in the absence of Air Commodore W.E.L. Wilson at ABDACOM. Praised for his actions on February 19, 1942, he went on to higher commands in the South West Pacific Area.

The Navy's Captain Edward Penry Thomas migrated to Australia from England and enlisted in the Royal Australian Navy in March 1931. Arriving in Darwin as Naval Officer in Charge he quickly made his presence felt. Described as a martinet he was also known as "Uncle Penry" or "God" and was a source of considerable friction in the Darwin Defence Coordination Committee. Responsible for Darwin harbor and shipping, Thomas was expecting an attack but failed to address problems associated with berthing and anchorages. A heavy loss of lives and vessels resulted. Thomas was replaced by Commodore C.J. Pope the following day, though this change had been decided the previous month.

Probably the most significant of those who defended Darwin on February 19, 1942 was **Maj. Floyd J. Pell** and even then his presence was

A fine study of Second Lt. (as he was at that time) Floyd J. Pell during his advance flying training course at Kelly Field. Graduating on October 5, 1938, he was rated as an "Airplane Pilot." (NARA via William H. Bartsch)

fortuitous. A native of Ogden Utah, Floyd Joachim Pell was appointed to the Military Academy at West Point in July 1933 and after graduating he undertook flying training from October 1937 to June 1938 before transferring to the Air Corps. He underwent further training at the Advanced Flying School attack course at Kelly Field, Texas. Promoted to captain on September 9, 1940, Pell went on to serve as engineering officer, group adjutant and deputy commander air of the 34th Bombardment Squadron, the 17th Bombardment Group, 34th Attack Squadron and General Headquarters. He was appointed operations officer for 4th Composite Group and HQ Squadron of the 20th Air Base Group at Nichols Field in the Philippines and in September 1941 he conducted a survey of facilities in Australia's north as part of a plan to establish a ferry route to the Philippines. In November 1941 he had flown to Darwin as a follow-up. Promoted to major on January 30, 1942 he was serving as air officer at Base Section 3 in Brisbane when he was ordered to form the 33rd Pursuit Squadron (Provisional).

THE JAPANESE

With the attacks on Pearl Harbor and Wake Island behind them, the Japanese plan to attack Darwin was assigned to a large carrier strike force, the *Kido Butai* under **VAdm. Chuichi Nagumo**.

A native of Yamagata Prefecture, Chuichi Nagumo graduated from the Imperial Japanese Navy Academy in 1908, and later from the Naval War College. He studied in Europe and the United States and was an adherent of

RIGHT
A leading Val pilot aboard the *Akagi*, Lt. Zenji Abe participated in the Pearl Harbor, Darwin and Ceylon attacks as a *shotai* leader under the Val element leader, Lt. Takehiko Chihaya.

LEFT
Highly respected as a leader, Mitsuo Fuchida led the Pearl Harbor, Wake Island, Darwin and Ceylon attacks from the *Akagi* before being wounded at Midway and spending the remainder of the war as a staff officer.

the role of naval vessels in surface actions, with little appreciation of the potential of aircraft. Nagumo served on a variety of vessels ranging from gunboats to cruisers and, later, on administrative duties, before being appointed Commander-in-Chief of the First Air Fleet, the Imperial Japanese Navy's main aircraft carrier force, on April 10, 1941. Despite his opposition to the attack on Pearl Harbor he oversaw the operation but his overly cautious nature saw him withdraw instead of launching a third attack and seeking the American carriers, much to the frustration of Adm. Isoroku Yamamoto, who failed to censure him. Following later successes at Wake Island, Darwin and the Indian Ocean raids the end came for Nagumo and the *Kido Butai* at Midway on June 4, 1942.

Nagumo's over-cautious nature was tempered by his officers, and **Cdr. Mitsuo Fuchida** in particular. A native of Nara Prefecture, Fuchida graduated from the Naval Academy at Eta Jima as a midshipman in 1924, going on to specialize in horizontal bombing; he later became an instructor in the technique. Assigned to the *Kaga* in 1929 and later the Sasebo *Kokutai*, he was promoted to lieutenant commander in 1936 and saw combat over China while serving aboard the *Kaga* in 1937. Fuchida was assigned to the *Akagi* as air group commander, or *Hikotaicho*, following graduation from the Naval Staff College in 1939. He was promoted to commander in late 1941 before leading the attacks on Pearl Harbor, Wake Island and Darwin.

Fuchida was in good company. Joining the Darwin raid as one of the aces of the Imperial Japanese Navy was **Lt. Cdr. Takashige Egusa** [Ekusa] an advocate of dive-bombing and the Navy's leading dive-bomber pilot along with the experienced fighter pilot, **Lt. Cdr. Shigeru Itaya.**

Takashige Egusa [Ekusa] was a native of Hiroshima Prefecture. He entered the Navy in April 1927 and graduated 59th of his class of 113 students of Class 58 in November 1930. From March 1931 he travelled to China, Hong Kong, Singapore, India, Greece, Italy and France aboard the training ship *Yakumo*. He was a November 1933 graduate of the 24th Flight Student Class and joined the carrier *Hosho* in April 1934. Originally a torpedo or horizontal bomber pilot he transferred to dive-bombers and served with the Tateyama and Saeki *Kokutai*, where he became a division leader (*Buntaicho*). Assigned to *Ryujo* as *Hikotaicho* in 1937 and later as an instructor, he was assigned to *Soryu* as the dive-bomber leader in August 1941. Promoted to lieutenant commander in October, he led the Vals on the Pearl Harbor, Wake Island and Darwin raids.

A native of Saga Prefecture, Shigeru Itaya joined the Navy in April 1926 and graduated from the Naval Academy's Engineering College Class 57 with honours in 1929. He served aboard the old 1890s cruiser and training ship *Iwate* (or *Asama*) and later graduated as a fighter pilot from the 23rd Class Aviation Students in July 1933. Assigned to *Ryujo* as a lieutenant in November 1936, he became *Buntaicho* of the carrier fighter group before assignment to *Hiryu* in January 1940 where he became *Hikotaicho* of its fighter group. Assigned to *Akagi* as wing leader in April 1941, he was promoted to lieutenant commander in November and led the fighter group on the Pearl Harbor, Wake Island and Darwin raids.

Seen as overly cautious, VAdm. Chuichi Nagumo failed to mount a third attack on Pearl Harbor, much to the displeasure of Adm. Isoroku Yamamoto. However, he was prepared to launch a second attack against Darwin on February 19, 1942, possibly as atonement.

The planner of both the Pearl Harbor and Darwin raids, and a classmate of Fuchida's at the Naval Academy, **Minoru Genda** was a native of Hiroshima Prefecture. He joined the Navy in 1924 and graduated from the 52nd Class at the Naval Academy and the 19th Aviation Student Class as a fighter pilot in November 1929. Assigned to the carrier *Akagi* in 1931, he formed an aerobatic team, "Genda's Flying Circus," which gave demonstrations throughout Japan. Following service in China during 1937, he was appointed as senior flying instructor at Yokosuka *Kokutai* and in 1940 he was assigned the role of military attaché in Britain. Following his return to Japan in February 1941 and meeting with Adm. Yamamoto, the plans for an attack on Pearl Harbor, which Genda had first envisaged in 1933, were put in motion. Genda took no part in the raids but analyzed their successes and any failures that might provide lessons for the future, including the attacks on Darwin and later Colombo, Ceylon, in April 1942.

OPPOSING FORCES

THE JAPANESE STRIKE FORCE

For the attack on Darwin the Japanese had assembled a large strike force, the *Kido Butai*, which included the carriers *Akagi*, Nagumo's flagship, and *Kaga* making up Carrier Division 1 (*Dai 1 Koku Sentai*), whilst *Hiryu* and *Soryu* made up *Dai 2*. Each carrier had an established strength of 63–72 aircraft comprising 27 Nakajima B5N2 Kate level bombers, 18 Aichi D3A1 Val dive-bombers and 18 Mitsubishi A6M2 Zeke fighters: a total of 432 aircraft with reserves. The carriers had also taken on 14 B5N2 Kates, 18 D3A1 Vals and 10 A6M2 Zekes from *Zuikaku* and *Shokaku* of Carrier Division 5 at Truk as the two returned to Japan.

The carrier-borne aircraft were manned by experienced pilots and crews, around 80 percent of whom had participated in the Pearl Harbor attacks, with very few as experienced as the attack leader, Fuchida.

The escorting surface protection force for Nagumo's carriers was a large one comprising the heavy cruisers *Tone* and *Chikuma* of Cruiser Division 8 and the light cruiser *Abukuma* of Destroyer Squadron 1. Seven destroyers, including *Urakaze*, *Isokaze*, *Tanikaze*, *Hamakaze*, all of Destroyer Division 17, along with *Kasumi* and *Shiranuhi* of Destroyer Division 18 and *Ariake* and *Yugure* of Destroyer Division 27, provided a screen against submarines. The Takao-class cruisers, *Takao* and *Maya*, of Cruiser Division 4 completed the task force after having sailed from Palau on February 16, while farther out as "distant cover" were the battleships *Hiei* and *Kirishima* of Battleship Division 3.

Launched at Kure Naval Arsenal on December 23, 1935, *Soryu* – "Blue Dragon" – had a complement of 72 aircraft. As part of Carrier Division 2 (*Dai 2 Koku Sentai*), she was involved in the Pearl Harbor, Wake Island, Darwin and Ceylon raids before being sunk at Midway.

Three remaining submarines of Submarine Squadron 6, *I-121*, *I-122* and *I-123* were also grouped with the force. Another of their squadron, *I-124*, had been sunk with the loss of all hands off Bathurst Island north of Darwin following a close-in engagement with HMAS *Deloraine* on January 21.

At the newly acquired bases at Kendari in the Celebes and at Laha opposite Ambon, the units that were to carry out the noon raid on Darwin were both experienced, having served over China and South East Asia. Formed at Kanoya on Kyushu on April 1, 1936, and initially equipped with Mitsubishi G3M1 Nell bombers, Kanoya *Kokutai* served in China from August 1937. Based at Hankow, the unit was assigned to the 11th *Koku Kantai* on January 15, 1941 and participated in attacks on Chunking and Chingtu under the direction of China Area Fleet as part of Operation *102*. Returning to Japan on September 2 the unit, re-equipped with Mitsubishi G4M1 Betty bombers, was assigned to the 21st *Koku Sentai*. On November 22 the unit moved to Taichu on Formosa and 12 days later it was ordered to send half its strength to Saigon in response to information that the British capital ships HMS *Prince of Wales* and HMS *Repulse* were heading for Singapore.

Hiryu – "Flying Dragon" – was launched at the Yokosuka Naval Arsenal on November 16, 1937 and had a complement of 73 aircraft. As part of *Dai 2 Koku Sentai*, she was involved in the same actions as *Soryu*, including support for operations in the Dutch East Indies, before being sunk at Midway.

Between December 2 and 5, 36 G4M1 Bettys of the 1st, 2nd and 3rd *Chutai* moved to Saigon under Capt. Naoshiro Fujiyoshi, leaving the 4th, 5th and 6th *Chutai* on Formosa under Lt. Cdr. Toshiie Irisa. On December 7 the unit was again on the move, this time to Thu Dao Moi near Saigon from where it was to attack the British Eastern Fleet (Force Z) under RAdm. Sir Tom Phillips. Planned for December 9, Kanoya *Kokutai* was assigned to carry out torpedo strikes. Following attacks by aircraft of the Genzan and Mihoro *Kokutai*, the Bettys of Kanoya *Kokutai* finished off the capital ships off the Malayan coast.

While the main unit then mounted attacks on Borneo and Singapore, the Formosa detachment was involved in attacks on airfields in the Philippines before deploying to Palau on December 18 and on to Davao eight days later. Ambon was attacked on January 7 and again on the 15th and 16th before the unit moved to Menado on January 21 and on to the newly captured airfield at Kendari six days later. On February 3 Irisa led 27 Bettys against Madioen on Java and the following day the unit participated in a strike on Adm. Karel Doorman's Combined Striking Force off Madoera Island. Attacks by 1 *Kokutai* Mitsubishi G3M2 Nells and Bettys of both Kanoya and Takao *Kokutai* damaged a number of ships. On February 19, 27 Bettys of Kanoya *Ku* took off from Kendari at 0635hrs, Tokyo time. Led by Lt. Cdr. Irisa, the force headed for Darwin. Five minutes later Lt. Cdr. Takeo Ozaki led 27 G3M2 Nells of 1 *Kokutai* from Ambon and headed for a rendezvous point en route to Darwin.

1 *Kokutai* had formed at Kanoya in southern Japan on April 10, 1941 with Nell bombers. Assigned to the 21st *Koku Sentai*, the unit deployed briefly to Hankow in central China during July. Returning to Kanoya it then moved to Hoihun (Haikow) on Hainan Island on October 24 before moving its 36 Nells to Tainan on November 18 to prepare for operations over the Philippines. From December 8 the unit carried out attacks on Clark Field before moving to Jolo Island on January 2, 1942, back to Tainan and on to Menado via Davao from January 26, to Kendari on the 31st and Ambon on February 9. From its arrival in the North Western Area of Operations (NWA) the unit was active in attacking land and sea targets. Lt. Cdr. Takeo Ozaki led an attack on Malang on February 3 and they joined in the attack on the 4th off Madoera Island. Attacks by the Nells of 1 *Kokutai* and Bettys of both Kanoya and Takao *Kokutai* followed, damaging a number of ships. On February 16, 36 Nells attacked the USS *Houston* convoy heading to Timor from Darwin, forcing it to return to port. Four days later 27 Nells of 1 *Kokutai* joined Kanoya *Kokutai* in the noon raid on Darwin's RAAF Station.

On February 16, the USS *Houston* convoy bound for Timor was attacked by 36 Mitsubishi G3M2 Nells of 1 *Kokutai*. From beneath the bomb spray, *Houston* kept up antiaircraft fire, with few casualties as a result. ("Bud" Guimond)

THE ALLIED DEFENCES

Facing the Japanese advances across the NEI were Dutch air and ground forces, including some 40,000 Dutch troops and 100,000 native troops most of whom were located on Java and poorly equipped, while their only available aircraft were obsolete Martin B-10 light bombers, Curtiss-Wright Hawk 75 and CW-21 fighters along with Brewster B339 (Buffalo) fighters. The Dutch Navy had a number of PBY Catalinas.

The Australians had No. 2 Squadron and its Hudson bombers at Koepang on Timor, along with RAAF support units and the army's "Sparrow Force" comprising infantry, artillery, antitank, engineers, signals, supply and maintenance units. At Laha opposite Ambon, No. 13 Squadron and its Hudsons were in action against the Japanese, while the Ambon Garrison, "Gull Force," and its 1,090 troops fought a losing battle. Number 13 Squadron withdrew to Darwin on January 31; Gull Force and a few Dutch defenders were overrun and three days later they were forced to surrender. The Hudsons of No. 2 Squadron lasted a further two weeks before flying out late on February 18; Sparrow Force fought on for a further four days losing 84 men killed before surrendering on the 23rd.

The Americans rushed aircraft to Java, ferrying B-17s and LB-30 Liberators of the 19th and 7th Bombardment Groups via Darwin and Batchelor, along with Douglas A-24 dive-bombers of the 27th Bombardment Group, while a number of stopgap squadrons, the 17th, 20th and 3rd Pursuit Squadrons (Provisional) equipped with P-40 fighters were hastily formed and trained in Brisbane before flying on to Java. The British contributed troops and aircraft including antiaircraft units, while Nos. 84, 204, 211 and 605 Squadrons along with Nos. 27, 34 and 62 Squadrons of 255 Group and their Vickers Vildebeests, Blenheims and Hurricanes all fought a losing battle.

ABDACOM enjoyed few victories, most of those in the air, but attacks by Dutch aircraft and the Dutch and US Navies against a Japanese invasion fleet at Balikpapan on January 23 and 24 cost the enemy six transports. Despite these losses, resistance by Dutch troops and their partial destruction of the oilfield, the Japanese gained control of the commodity they desperately needed, but, with a lack of suitable transport and attacks by submarines, only a trickle ever reached Japan.

A pair of Glenn Martin B-10 bombers of the Dutch Air Force during a May 1941 visit to Darwin, where they were welcomed by the RAAF Station Commander, Group Captain Charles Eaton.

DARWIN'S DEFENCES

Over the years since 1942, Darwin's defences have been criticized as being neglected, unprepared and inadequate. However they were, in fact, as prepared as they could be and the military had enjoyed a build-up of forces in the area from the mid-1920s when its role as a strategic naval facility was mooted and abandoned. Instead Darwin was consigned to the role of a naval refuelling facility as part of the failed "Singapore Strategy" and the construction of a series of naval oil storage tanks was commenced in 1924. Fortifications at East and Emery Points followed and the installation of four 6-inch guns and 3-inch antiaircraft guns was completed by late 1937 while an anti-submarine boom net was laid across the harbour; the longest in the world, it stretched 4 miles from East to West Points. Naval facilities including a boom wharf and maintenance facilities followed.

Construction of the RAAF Station commenced in 1938, while the Civil 'Drome served as a temporary base for No. 12 Squadron. By June 1, 1940, the RAAF Station was complete enough to be declared operational and a new squadron, No. 13, was formed that day. Larrakeyah Barracks, hutted military camps at Stuart Park and Winnellie on Darwin's eastern outskirts and naval facilities at Coonawarra and HMAS *Melville* were constructed, while a military hospital, 119 Australian General Hospital (AGH), was also established. A reticulated water system was completed and the first water flowed from the newly constructed Manton Dam 37 miles south of Darwin in March 1941.

Antiaircraft defences were modernized with all but two of the old 3-inch guns relocated to Batchelor airfield in 1941 and replaced by the new 3.7-inch quick firing guns. 14 Heavy Anti-Aircraft Battery (HAA) established sites on Darwin's football field, the Oval, at McMillans Farm north of the RAAF Station and at Fannie Bay while 2 HAA Battery established a battery at Berrimah. By late 1941, 16 of the 3.7-inch guns and two 3-inch guns along with Light Anti-Aircraft Machine Gun (LAAMG) Troops and the searchlights of 1/54 Anti-Aircraft Searchlight Battery (AASL) were sited around Darwin. A further AA site was under construction near Darwin's old Quarantine

Formed on June 1, 1940, No. 13 Squadron RAAF was equipped with Lockheed Hudson bombers. Here No. 13 Squadron Hudsons fly over Darwin. The Civil 'Drome and racecourse are at centre left and East Point (Port War) bottom centre. (Ken Nicolson)

Darwin's antiaircraft defenses, February 19, 1942

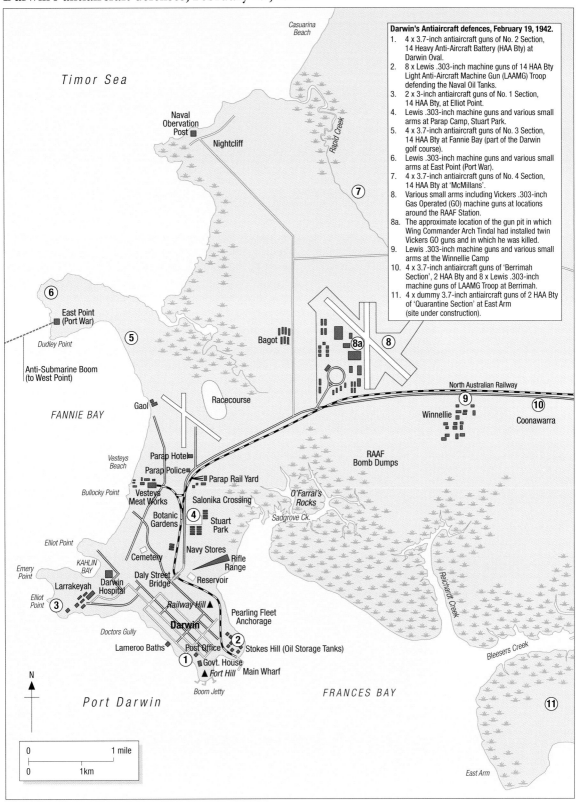

Darwin's Antiaircraft defences, February 19, 1942.

1. 4 x 3.7-inch antiaircraft guns of No. 2 Section, 14 Heavy Anti-Aircraft Battery (HAA Bty) at Darwin Oval.
2. 8 x Lewis .303-inch machine guns of 14 HAA Bty Light Anti-Aircraft Machine Gun (LAAMG) Troop defending the Naval Oil Tanks.
3. 2 x 3-inch antiaircraft guns of No. 1 Section, 14 HAA Bty, at Elliot Point.
4. Lewis .303-inch machine guns and various small arms at Parap Camp, Stuart Park.
5. 4 x 3.7-inch antiaircraft guns of No. 3 Section, 14 HAA Bty at Fannie Bay (part of the Darwin golf course).
6. Lewis .303-inch machine guns and various small arms at East Point (Port War).
7. 4 x 3.7-inch antiaircraft guns of No. 4 Section, 14 HAA Bty at 'McMillans'.
8. Various small arms including Vickers .303-inch Gas Operated (GO) machine guns at locations around the RAAF Station.
8a. The approximate location of the gun pit in which Wing Commander Arch Tindal had installed twin Vickers GO guns and in which he was killed.
9. Lewis .303-inch machine guns and various small arms at the Winnellie Camp
10. 4 x 3.7-inch antiaircraft guns of 'Berrimah Section', 2 HAA Bty and 8 x Lewis .303-inch machine guns of LAAMG Troop at Berrimah.
11. 4 x dummy 3.7-inch antiaircraft guns of 2 HAA Bty of 'Quarantine Section' at East Arm (site under construction).

Casuarina Beach

Timor Sea

Naval Obervation Post

Nightcliff

Rapid Creek

⑦

⑥
East Point (Port War)

Dudley Point

⑤

Bagot

⑧ᵃ ⑧

Anti-Submarine Boom (to West Point)

North Australian Railway

FANNIE BAY

Gaol

Racecourse

⑨ ⑩
Winnellie   Coonawarra

Vesteys Beach

Parap Hotel

Parap Police

Parap Rail Yard

Bullocky Point

Vesteys Meat Works

Salonika Crossing

O'Farral's Rocks

RAAF Bomb Dumps

Sadgrove Ck.

Botanic Gardens

④ Stuart Park

Elliot Point

Cemetery

Navy Stores

Emery Point

KAHLIN BAY

Larrakeyah

Darwin Hospital

Daly Street Bridge

Reservoir

Rifle Range

Reichardt Creek

Elliot Point

③

Railway Hill ▲

Pearling Fleet Anchorage

Doctors Gully

Darwin

Lameroo Baths

Post Office ②

① Govt. House

▲ Fort Hill   Main Wharf

Stokes Hill (Oil Storage Tanks)

Bleesers Creek

N

Boom Jetty

FRANCES BAY

⑪

Port Darwin

0	1 mile
0	1km

East Arm

LEFT
A 3.7-inch antiaircraft gun and crew at 14 HAA Battery's Fannie Bay site, the first to fire on February 19, 1942 when Gun Sergeant Laurie Huby fired a warning shot to an incoming Hudson which failed to flash its identification lights.

RIGHT
The well dug-in and camouflaged 3.7-inch guns of 14 HAA Battery at the Oval site. The Administrator's Residence (Government House) is at left overlooking Fort Hill and the main jetty.

Station at East Arm. With some 10,000 troops including infantry, artillery, engineers, searchlight, machine-gun and antitank units in the area, Darwin was arguably as well defended as it could have been in light of the effects of the Depression and government neglect. The same could not be said for its aerial defenses, however.

While Darwin's RAAF Station was a modern facility, the Air Force itself had been subservient to the Army and Navy as the "third brother" and neglected by successive governments; its equipment was lacking in every respect. When the Japanese struck, there were no RAAF fighters available despite P-40 Kittyhawks being on order. The only aircraft remotely resembling a fighter was the Australian designed and produced Wirraway. More effective in the light bombing and army cooperation roles, the Wirraways of No. 24 Squadron had been decimated over Rabaul when they had attempted to intercept Japanese raiders a month previously. The Wirraways of No. 12 Squadron based at Darwin's Civil 'Drome and at Batchelor, 62 miles south would have fared no better. Fortunately they were denied the chance.

Declared operational on June 1, 1940 the RAAF Station boasted two large hangars, workshops, a hospital, transport section, messes and recreational facilities. At left is the site of 119 Australian General Hospital, before it moved to Berrimah where it was strafed during the first attack.

THE AMERICAN PROVISIONAL SQUADRONS

That Darwin had any fighter defence at all on February 19 was at best fortuitous and at worst the result of decisions made in the increasingly critical situation in which the Allies found themselves in the face of rapid Japanese victories in the NEI.

The presence over Darwin of ten P-40Es of the 33rd Pursuit Squadron (Provisional) under Maj. Floyd "Slugger" Pell was also their downfall. Turned back by deteriorating weather, Pell was forced to return from an early morning flight to Timor and Java to join ABDACOM. The inexperienced pilots were no match for the Japanese and of the Allied aircraft lost, nine were American P-40 fighters, all as a result of aerial combat, with four pilots killed and the unit decimated in a matter of minutes.

The 33rd Pursuit Squadron (Provisional) had arrived in Darwin on February 15, following an eventful trip north from Port Pirie in South Australia and losing a number of aircraft and pilots along the way. Its presence at Darwin had begun two months previously with the diversion of a convoy bound for the Philippines.

On December 22, 1941, the USS *Pensacola* convoy docked in Brisbane. Aboard the *Holbrook*, *Meigs* and *Admiral Halstead* were some 2,600 USAAC personnel including 48 pilots, the US Army's 147th and 148th Field Artillery Regiments, elements of the 7th Bombardment Group and Gen. Claire Chennault's American Volunteer Group (AVG) en route to China. Eighteen P-40E fighters, 52 Douglas A-24s assigned to the 27th Bombardment Group (Light), seven million rounds of .50-inch ammunition, 5,000 bombs, general-purpose weapons and several thousand drums of aviation fuels, oils and Prestone coolant completed the manifest. The *Holbrook* sailed shortly after, bound for its intended destination with the 147th and 148th Regiments aboard. However Gen. George H. Brett followed up a directive from the Chief of Staff Gen. George C. Marshall that Darwin be used as a base and diverted the vessel north, where she arrived on January 5.

At Brisbane the crated A-24 and P-40 aircraft were transported to RAAF Station Amberley, where they were assembled by American and Australian

No. 12 Squadron arrived in Darwin from September 5, 1939 and was initially accommodated at the Civil 'Drome, where its Wirraways flew patrols over the Darwin area. Three of the type are seen over Darwin town, with Sadgroves Creek in the background.

mechanics. By January 12, 15 P-40s were completed and test flown while more were arriving; the USS *President Polk* arrived on January 12 with 55 aircraft, the SS *Mormac Sun* brought 67, the *Mariposa* 19 and *Coolidge* 32. Between January 12 and February 2, 1942, 173 P-40s were assembled ready for assignment to the new Provisional squadrons being formed to bolster American forces in the Philippines.

The first to form was the 17th Pursuit Squadron (Provisional). On January 14 Maj. Charles A. Sprague was instructed: "organize the 17th Pursuit Squadron (Provisional) with 17 P-40E type airplanes, 17 Pilots, 17 Crew chiefs, 17 Armourers, 1 Line Chief and First Sergeant, and three Radiomen," the unit diarist recorded. Two days later the unit was ready to leave for the Philippines. However, the Japanese had severed the air route and instead they were ordered to Java. Led by Sprague and Captain Walter Coss they flew out in two groups on the 17th. Two P-40s did not make it out of Queensland. At Rockhampton Lt. Carl Giess ground looped 40-667 while Lt. Bryan Brown's landing gear collapsed on landing at Cloncurry, damaging 40-663. A third aircraft, 41-5334, flown by Lt. Joe Kruzel, had its landing gear collapse at Darwin and was moved to the 12 Squadron hangar. On January 26 the remaining aircraft flew on to Java with Kruzel flying the aircraft of Lt. Ben Irvin who had fallen ill.

The next unit to form was the 20th Pursuit Squadron (Provisional) with Lt. William Lane Jr. the commander. Twenty-five aircraft departed Amberley under escort of a B-24A, 40-2374, on January 20, losing two en route; one flown by Lt. Bernard Oliver scraped a wing landing in crosswind at Charleville while Lt. George Parker had undercarriage problems and crashed at Cloncurry. Lieutenant Allison W. Strauss flew in a replacement aircraft to Charleville and two flights eventually left Darwin in heavy rain on February 4 after being delayed by monsoonal weather. The first flight lost eight aircraft

American and Australian air force personnel inspecting the Allison engine of a P-40E at the RAAF Station Amberley assembly depot. (David Vincent)

at Bali: three in combat, two to strafing and the remainder in accidents. The second flight lost two aircraft when they crash landed at Lombok. Only 15 eventually made it through to Java.

The last to fly the route via Darwin was the 3rd Pursuit Squadron (Provisional). Commanded by Lt. Grant Mahoney, the unit was hastily manned by newly arrived and inexperienced pilots, along with what veterans of the Philippines were available. Twenty-four aircraft in two flights led by Mahoney and Strauss left for Darwin on February 6, losing one at Charleville when Lt. Ralph Martin's P-40 was flipped over by a sudden gust of wind, while another was forced to turn back for Amberley. Two were lost on landing at Daly Waters while Lt. Oscar Handy crashed on landing at Darwin and two others were sent back to Amberley. When the 3rd left for Java, two pilots and their unserviceable aircraft remained: Lts. Robert J. Buel and Robert G. Oestreicher. They were to fly on once expected reinforcements arrived. They never came and the two remained at Darwin.

Only eight aircraft of the 3rd Pursuit Squadron (Provisional) eventually reached their destination. Of the first flight, seven pilots, low on fuel and lost, crashed or baled out along the Timor coast. Six were picked up by the RAAF and one was killed. The other flight reached Java, but losses by the 3rd and the other Provisional squadrons caused a major rethink by the Americans. In the event, the Japanese solved the problem for them when they invaded Timor and the route was severed.

The fifth of the Provisional Squadrons, the 13th, was formed by a Philippines veteran, Captain Boyd "Buzz" Wagner, in early February using whatever pilots were available. Along with the 33rd Pursuit Squadron (Provisional), Wagner was ordered from Amberley to join up with the USS *Langley* convoy at Fremantle in Western Australia by Brig. Gen. Julian Barnes on February 10. They were the last of the provisional squadrons to form,

Lieutenant Oestreicher and his P-40E at Darwin after he painted the sharkmouth on February 13, 1942. The photo was one of a few items salvaged when Oestreicher crashed at Cloncurry, Queensland, on October 8.

with P-40s landed from the USAT *Monroe* on January 30 and hastily assembled and test flown.

The 33rd Pursuit Squadron (Provisional) formed at Amberley under newly promoted Maj. Floyd "Slugger" Pell on February 4, 1942, in compliance with orders issued by Headquarters United States Army Forces in Australia (USAFIA). At a pilots' meeting Pell picked 24 pilots from the rapidly dwindling supply; only one, Lt. Gerry Keenan, a veteran of the Philippines, was experienced, while the others were barely out of flying school. Even Pell, an experienced fighter pilot who had served in the Philippines, had no combat experience.

33rd Pursuit Squadron (Provisional) pilots, Darwin, February 19, 1942

Number	Rank	Name	Unit assigned from	Date enlisted	Class/Flying school	Origins, date of birth & date of death as at 2013	Aircraft tail number
O-20701	Maj.	Pell, Floyd J.	HQ USAFFE	12.6.37 West Point	38-C Kelly	Ogden UT DOB 29.12.1913 KIA 19.2.1942	3 – had 28 on 19.2.42
O-427453	2nd Lt.	McMahon, Robert F.	21st P.Sq	8.2.41	41-G Kelly	Mitchell SD DOB 1918	22 – on 15.2.42
O-427738	2nd Lt.	Hughes, Charles W.		8.2.41	41-G Kelly	Hamilton OH DOB 1918 KIA 19.2.1942	94
O-429978	2nd Lt.	Rice, Burt H.	14th P.Sq	29.9.41	41-H Mather	Reno NV DOB 8.3.1914 DOD 28.11.1967	31
O-327496	2nd Lt.	Glover, John G.	35th P.Gp	8.2.41	41-G Kelly	Fargo ND DOB 21.3.1915 DOD 13.5.1990	36
O-416707	2nd Lt.	Peres, Jack R.	21st P.Sq	31.12.40	41-F Kelly	Santa Barbara CA DOB 5.3.1920 KIA 19.2.1942	189
O-425042	2nd Lt.	Perry, Elton S.	34th P.Sq	31.12.40	41-F Kelly	Phoenix AZ DOB 1917 KIA 19.2.1942	51
O-430006	2nd Lt.	Wiecks, Max R.	14th P.Sq	15.3.41	41-H Mather	Dallas TX DOB 18.8.1915 DOD 13.10.2004	9
O-430001	2nd Lt.	Walker, William R.	14th P.Gp	15.3.41	41-H Mather	Jacksonville TX DOB 1919 DOD 25.5.1944	46
O-421298	2nd Lt.	Oestreicher, Robert G.	3rd P.Sq	22.11.40	41-E Brooks	Columbus OH DOB 29.7.1917 DOD 10.1.1991	43
O-382764	2nd Lt.	Vaught, Robert H.	14th P.Gp	29.9.41	41-H Mather	Los Angeles CA DOB 1919 KIA 5.3.1943	28 (taken by Pell)

Kelly Field (Air Force Base) – near San Antonio, Texas. Formed 1917, closed 2001.

Brooks Field (Air Force Base) – near San Antonio, Texas. Formed 1918, closed 2011.

Mather Field (Air Force Base) – near Sacramento, California. Formed 1918, closed 1993.

The designation of the classes indicates the year and month. 41-H denotes August 1941.

ORDERS OF BATTLE

IMPERIAL JAPANESE NAVY

Carrier force – *Kido Butai*

Carrier Division 1 – *Dai 1 Koku Sentai*

Akagi – flagship of VAdm. Chuichi Nagumo

Kaga

Carrier Division 2 – *Dai 2 Koku Sentai*

Hiryu

Soryu

Escorting protection force

Heavy cruisers *Tone* and *Chikuma* – Cruiser Division 8. Each
carried up to six Nakajima E8N1 (Dave) floatplanes

Light cruiser *Abukuma* – Destroyer Squadron 1

Cruisers *Takao* and *Maya* – Cruiser Division 4

Destroyers *Urakaze, Isokaze, Tanikaze* and *Hamakaze* – Destroyer
Division 17

Destroyers *Kasumi* and *Shiranuhi* – Destroyer Division 18

Destroyers *Ariake* and *Yugure* – Destroyer 27

Distant Cover 3

Battleships *Hiei* and *Kirishima* – Battleship Division 3

Submarine force

I-121, I-122 and *I-123* – Submarine Squadron 6

Carrier-borne air attack element

Nakajima B5N2 level bomber (Kate)

Akagi – 18, *Kaga* – 18, *Hiryu* – 27 and *Soryu* – 18

Aichi D3A1 dive-bomber (Val)

Akagi – 18, *Kaga* – 18, *Hiryu* – 17 and *Soryu* – 18

Mitsubishi A6M2 fighter (Zeke)

Akagi – 9, *Kaga* - 9, *Hiryu* – 9 and *Soryu* – 9 assigned as top cover
over Darwin

Land-based air attack element

Mitsubishi G3M2 bomber (Nell) of 1 *Kokutai*, 21st *Koku Sentai* –
27

Mitsubishi G4M1 bomber (Betty) of Kanoya *Kokutai*, 21st *Koku
Sentai* – 27

ALLIED FORCES – DARWIN

AUSTRALIAN ARMY – MAJOR UNITS

Headquarters 7 Military District

23 Infantry Brigade

2/4 Machine Gun Battalion

2/4 Pioneer Battalion

2/21 Infantry Battalion

2/40 Infantry Battalion

19 Infantry Battalion

27 Infantry Battalion

43 Infantry Battalion

2/14 Field Regiment

19 Machine Gun Regiment

2/1 Heavy Artillery Battery

**Emery Point, West Point and Emery Point Heavy Artillery
Batteries**

2 Heavy Anti-Aircraft Battery

14 Heavy Anti-Aircraft Battery

14 Anti-Tank Battery

18 Field Battery

1/54 Anti-Aircraft Searchlight Battery

UNITED STATES ARMY

147th Field Artillery Regiment

148th Field Artillery Regiment – aboard the ships *Portmar* and
Tulagi during raid

ROYAL AUSTRALIAN NAVY – MAJOR VESSELS

Corvettes – HMAS *Deloraine, Katoomba* and *Warrnambool*

Minesweeper – HMAS *Gunbar*

Sloops - HMAS *Swan* and *Warrego*

Boom defense vessels – HMAS *Kangaroo, Karangi, Kara Kara* and
Koala

Depot ship – HMAS *Platypus*

Patrol boat – HMAS *Kiara*

UNITED STATES NAVY

Destroyer – USS *Peary*

Seaplane tender – USS *William B. Preston*

Consolidated PBY Catalina flying boats – three with two on
patrol

ROYAL AUSTRALIAN AIR FORCE

HQ North Western Area of Operations – at RAAF Station

Area Combined Headquarters – at RAAF Station

Lockheed Hudson bombers – nine of Nos. 2 and 13 Squadrons
at RAAF Station (eight at Daly Waters)

CAC Wirraway fighter/light bomber – five of No. 12 Squadron at
Parap Civil 'Drome (nine at Batchelor)

UNITED STATES ARMY AIR FORCES

Curtiss Wright P-40E fighters – ten of the 33rd Pursuit Squadron
(Provisional) at the RAAF Station

OPPOSING PLANS

DARWIN TARGETED

Following the devastating raids on Pearl Harbor, the lightning advances by Japanese forces throughout the Pacific and a desperate battle by the Allies' last hope for the Netherlands East Indies, Wavell's ABDACOM, it became evident that an attack on Australia was more a matter of when and not if. The neutralization of Darwin as an Allied base was imperative to Japanese plans for conquering the NEI with a view to the Java Campaign, and to the invasion of Bali on February 18 and 19 and Timor by Gen. Sadashi Doi's army on February 20.

On February 9, just eight weeks after the attacks on Pearl Harbor and six days prior to the fall of Singapore, the suggestion of a strike on Darwin by RAdm. Tamon Yamaguchi was followed up by the Southern Area Fleet Commander, VAdm. Nobutake Kondo, when he relayed Secret Telegraphic Order No. 92 to VAdm. Chuichi Nagumo, the commander of Carrier Divisions 1 and 2, *Dai 1* and *Dai 2*, *Koku Sentai* of the Mobile Fleet, the *Kido Butai* – the same force that had devastated Pearl Harbor.

In part Telegraphic Order No. 92 stated:

> Owing to our air attacks at the beginning of February, the enemy, with its main base in Java, lost most of its naval and air strength … it appears that a part of the enemy strength is already taking refuge in the vicinity of Port Darwin. Intelligence shows that part of the U.S. air reinforcements, together with British and Australian forces are based there. At an opportune time the carrier task forces will conduct mobile warfare, firstly in the Arafura Sea … to seek to annihilate the enemy strength in the Port Darwin area … for the surprise attacks on Darwin on February 19, the task force will advance to the Arafura Sea. After the surprise attack it will return [to Staring Bay southeast of Kendari] for supply.

At 1020hrs (1150 Darwin time) the following day, a Mitsubishi C5M2 Babs, one of six reconnaissance aircraft belonging to 3 *Kokutai*, took off from Ambon (Base 333) and headed for Darwin. "[A]fter stealthily reconnoitring over and taking photos of Port Darwin", the C5M2 Babs landed at 1720hrs Tokyo time. The crew of Petty Officer 3c (PO3c) Takahashi and Petty Officer 1c (PO1c) Yoshimaru Kizai reported, "There were two airports … in the northern suburb of Port Darwin. In the eastern airport [RAAF Station] five

The ABDACOM area of responsibility, February 1942

large planes and 20 small planes were spotted. Three fighters were flying guard over the city at the altitude of about 2,000 metres… The base for flying boats was located at the south-east corner of Port Darwin. Three flying boats were spotted there."

The Babs crew also reported at least 27 ships in the harbour and planning for the attack on February 19 proceeded.

Taken from a Mitsubishi C5M2 Babs of 3 *Kokutai* on March 4, 1942 (dated 17.3.4), this view of Darwin would also have been seen during the February 10 reconnaissance sortie.

Other parts of the Telegraphic Order No. 92 had also set mission profiles for both land-based and flying boat units in the area, while a further directive, V. Adm. Kondo's Telegraphic Order No. 53 of February 15 included added detail. Three days later the plan of attack was confirmed. The orders for the land-based bombers and flying boats of the 21st *Koku Sentai* (Air Flotilla) were:

1.   The land-based attack planes will attack the Port Darwin airport [RAAF Station] at 1130.
2.   The large flying boats will seek the enemy in the Arafura Sea AND Timor Sea areas with part of its large flying boat force… [and then] move the majority of the… force to Kupang.

With that the carriers began preparation for the attack on Darwin the following morning, while preparations also commenced at both 1 and Kanoya *Kokutai* on Ambon and at Kendari for their attack on the RAAF Station.

DARWIN – A WAITING GAME

Despite resistance on all fronts the dominoes were falling throughout the ABDACOM area. With a succession of Japanese victories in Malaya, Thailand, Singapore, the NEI, British Borneo and the Philippines, the "Malay Barrier" crumbled. The fall of Singapore on February 15, 1942 and the capture of over 60,000 Allied troops and equipment was a major loss described by Churchill as "the worst disaster and largest capitulation in British history."

The loss of Malaya and Singapore and the impending loss of the NEI effectively dislocated ABDACOM. Timor and Bali were targeted for invasion on February 19 and 20 and Java was close to collapse. Darwin was the only obstacle to Japan's plans and it was to be eliminated as a threat only four days after Singapore fell.

With the writing on the wall the Combined Chiefs of Staff in London cabled Wavell on February 21, authorizing him to close his headquarters and withdraw at his discretion. Stressing the need for a timely withdrawal they magnanimously allowed the Dutch to decide who should leave and who should stay. The following day they followed up with a cable directing that all personnel and units under arms continue to fight without any thought of evacuation. However, Air Force units which were able to operate outside Java should be withdrawn. The cable concluded, "With respect to people who cannot contribute to defence, [the] general policy should be to withdraw U.S. and Australian personnel to Australia."

Wavell closed his headquarters on February 25 and followed Brereton to India, handing control of the ABDA area to local commanders. With that, ABDACOM was effectively finished. The final nail was driven home with the destruction of RAdm. Karel Doorman's naval force in the battle of the Java Sea on February 27 and the battle of Sunda Strait over the following two days in which the Allies lost USS *Houston* and HMAS *Perth*.

ABDACOM formally ended with the surrender of the NEI on March 9, 1942. It had been in existence for a few short weeks during which it presided over one defeat after another. With very few successes on the board, its most notable was the guerrilla campaign waged against the Japanese by Australian infantry on Timor for almost 12 months after Japanese landings there on February 19, 1942: the day the Japanese devastated Darwin in two air raids.

In Darwin itself any plans effectively hinged on the future of ABDACOM. A Darwin Defence Plan had been implemented in April 1941 and was replaced by Brigadier W. Steele on July 10. This was again superseded by the Darwin Defence Scheme and the available forces dispersed in expectation of a Japanese attack – by land.

Civilians and non-essential personnel had been evacuated from December 10, 1941, leaving some 60 women in a military town. Over the period from December 15, 1941 to February 15, 1942, 1,414 left by sea, others travelled by road and the last by air on February 18.

An Air Raid Precautions group had been formed by volunteers and a Darwin Defence Coordination Committee had been established with representatives of the armed services, ARP and the Administrator of the Northern Territory, C.L.A. Abbott. Riven with internal politics it was described as a "Line of communication rather than a Line of command."

By February 1942, and with the military firmly in command, Darwin was looking north to the lightning advances by the Japanese on Java and the NEI. In an attempt to reinforce Timor's meager forces a convoy was sent under escort by USS *Houston*. Turned back by Japanese air attacks the convoy returned to an edgy Darwin on the evening of February 18.

At least 67 vessels of varying sizes were in Darwin harbor when 188 Japanese carrier-borne aircraft swept in from the southeast the following morning, Thursday February 19, 1942.

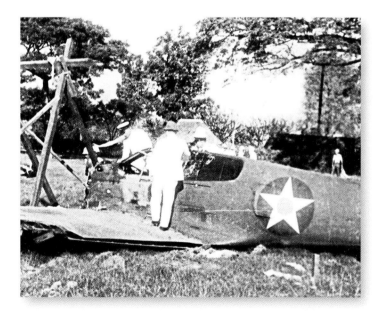

Following the surrender of the Netherlands East Indies, the Japanese were able to assess Allied equipment. A P-40 of one of the USAAF Provisional Squadrons is inspected by Japanese naval officers.

THE BATTLE

TO DARWIN – THE LONG FLIGHT NORTH

With his new squadron formed, Pell selected his flight commanders with himself leading, along with Lieutenants Keenan, Jack R. Peres and Robert F. McMahon. His pilots, some with only a few hours' flying experience, were rushed into flying combat tactics, formation flying and general flying, but were given no gunnery training. On February 10 Pell was ordered to Perth's Maylands Aerodrome to join the *Langley* at Fremantle. Staging through Richmond RAAF Station west of Sydney they were escorted by an RAAF Airspeed Oxford flown by Wg. Cdr. Mackey to No. 3 Bombing and Gunnery School at West Sale in Victoria on February 13. Local residents recalled a number landing on the main highway as they ran short of fuel.

The next leg of the journey, the short hop to Laverton RAAF Station, was little better. Only three landed there while 11 went on to the RAAF Station at Point Cook a few miles away. Lieutenant Charles Hughes force landed short of fuel at Point Cook some time later.

Continuing, the squadron got as far as Port Pirie before Pell received orders to fly 15 aircraft north to Darwin with the intention of deploying to Timor at a later date. In the meantime it was to provide fighter protection for Darwin- and Java-bound convoys. Keenan was ordered to continue with his flight to Perth and the ill-fated *Langley*.

Accidents took their toll during the flight to Darwin. Lieutenant Richard Pingree was forced to remain at Port Pirie for repairs but crashed shortly after takeoff and was killed on February 19, while another, Lt. Bryce Wilhite, was also forced to remain at Port Pirie with an unserviceable aircraft before being ordered to return to Amberley via Laverton. Staging

P-40s of "B" Flight, 13th Pursuit Squadron (Provisional) staging through RAAF Station Richmond west of Sydney during the flight to Perth. (Rick Hanning)

through Oodnadatta, Alice Springs and Daly Waters, Pell lost more aircraft. Lieutenant Jess Dore had a flat tyre at Alice Springs and Lt. David Latane also remained at the central Australian base while the remainder flew on.

Lieutenant Bob McMahon hit a grader on the strip during takeoff at Daly Waters, damaging the undercarriage and main spar of his aircraft, but elected to fly on to Darwin. Lieutenant Richard Suehr was forced to put his aircraft down approximately 37 miles south of Darwin near the Marrakai Track. Alerted by McMahon, the RAAF Station dispatched a Douglas A-24 of the USAAF's 27th Bombardment Group, which dropped food and supplies to Suehr. Landing in the dark the A-24 crashed on the Civil 'Drome and with its wings removed was transported to the RAAF Station for repairs the next day.

Meanwhile, Suehr spent his first night sleeping on the wing of his P-40, before heading north on foot. After walking for ten days, swimming a large river, avoiding crocodiles and buffaloes and finally locating the railway line, he was picked up by a train and taken to Darwin. His aircraft was later salvaged while Suehr himself was hospitalized for some months before flying in the New Guinea Campaign.

FIRST TO FALL

When Pell and his remaining aircraft landed at the RAAF Station late on February 15, they found Lt. Robert G. Oestreicher and his P-40 there. Oestreicher was the survivor of two 3rd Pursuit Squadron (Provisional) pilots stranded at Darwin when their aircraft went unserviceable on February 10. The other pilot, Lt. Robert J. "Blackie" Buel, was missing after being sent out to intercept a Japanese Kawanishi H6K4 Mavis flying boat off Bathurst Island earlier that day.

Second Lieutenant Robert J. "Blackie" Buel during his flight training at the Advanced Flying School at Stockton Field, California in 1941. (Katharine Buel Brothers via Bob Piper)

With the probability of Darwin being attacked and the situation on the NEI rapidly deteriorating, Japanese reconnaissance and patrols across Australia's north coast were expanded with the large H6K4 Mavis flying boats of Toko *Kokutai* flying long-range armed reconnaissance missions from their bases at Ambon and Ceram. On February 15, 1942, three Mavis took off from Ceram at 0626hrs on a patrol over the Arafura Sea to "find any convoy that might be leaving Darwin to reinforce Timor" former navigator Marekuni Takahara recalled. "A convoy was discovered at 1030 [and] was reported by radio… We were instructed to keep the vessels in sight."

The convoy was led by the American cruiser USS *Houston* shepherding seven vessels, including four transports sailing for Timor with reinforcements. The Mavis shadowed the convoy for another three

hours and it was reported to Darwin: "at 0215/Z/15 that a convoy … was being shadowed by an enemy Type-97 flying boat … when in position 12° 30' S 128° 45' E" (135 miles west of Darwin). At 0448Z/Z/15 a signal was received stating that the convoy was being bombed."

With fuel beginning to run low the Mavis turned for home, releasing 60kg bombs over the convoy, but causing no damage. Following the report of the attack on the convoy, the RAAF Station commander, Wg. Cdr. Sturt de B. Griffith, ordered the only available aircraft at his disposal to fly out and intercept the enemy aircraft. Oestreicher was reportedly out of contact and "Blackie" Buel was ordered out. Buel took off and headed for the last known position of the convoy as the *Mavis* turned for home. Relaxing after having bombed the convoy, the crew were about to have lunch when, "a single-engine fighter, which looked like a Spitfire, approached us from the front on the right," Takahara recalled, "the crew rushed to their posts and I … manned the 20-millimetre cannon in the tail."

Buel in his inexperience overflew the Mavis and came in from astern, where he was met with 20mm fire. In turn his fire had found its mark, severely wounding the radio operator, Flight Chief Petty Officer (FCPO) Kinichi Furakawa, and had set the flying boat on fire. Takahara recalled the aircraft diving and the pilot, Lt. Mirau, signaling "G-G-G" before the Mavis hit the water. The crew, including the badly wounded Furakawa, took to a life raft, though Furakawa died two days later and was buried at sea. The remainder, including Takahara, Mirau, the flight engineer, Akamoto and another crewman, Sichisima, drifted ashore on Melville Island on February 19 as the carrier-borne aircraft flew over on their way to attack Darwin.

Lieutenant Oestreicher reportedly carried out searches for Buel when he failed to return and flew over the Tiwi Islands the following day. It was all in vain; neither Buel nor his P-40, "54," have been located. He was the first to die in aerial combat over northern Australia.

Over the next 11 days the Mavis survivors roamed the beaches foraging for food and water before they were captured by Louis Paraptameli and four other Aboriginal men, while collecting crabs near Tikalarpin Creek (Calico Creek) on Melville Island on March 2. Handed over to Sergeant Les Powell of the 23rd Field Company Royal Australian Engineers, then preparing for the possible demolition of the Bathurst Island Mission airstrip, they were later transported to Darwin, Adelaide River and on to Cowra POW Camp in NSW.

On February 16, a C-53 carrying Pell's crew chiefs and mechanics landed at Darwin

Lieutenant Marekuni Takahara in flying gear, 1941. Visiting Darwin in 1992 he related being cared for at 119 Australian General Hospital at Adelaide River before being sent to Cowra POW camp. (Bob Piper)

Lieutenant Buel's P-40E "54" taken shortly before he was sent to the USS *Houston* convoy. Taken by RAAF fitter Ken Tinkler, it is the last known photo of the aircraft at Darwin. (Ken Tinkler)

Lieutenant Buel's P-40E over the USS *Houston* convoy. Directed towards the Japanese Mavis, he was not seen again and has never been located. ("Bud" Guimond)

along with their tool kits and spares. Whereas the pilots had previously carried out basic servicing with assistance by RAAF fitters, over the following two days the newly arrived ground crews carried out repairs and maintained the aircraft in readiness for the trip to Timor, while patrols were flown from Darwin out over the Timor Sea in what serviceable aircraft there were. Unserviceable aircraft left behind by other units were either cannibalized for spares or repaired to flying condition and, by the evening of the February 18, Pell had ten aircraft serviceable enough for the planned flight to Timor.

Following his accident at Daly Waters, Bob McMahon's P-40E, 41-5421, "Barhootee the Cootee," was written off at Darwin. An aircraft left behind by another unit was restored to flying condition and named "Barhootee the

Lieutenant Bob McMahon's second aircraft, "Barhootee the Cootee II"/"MAC" after his accident on February 18. RAAF Photographer, Sergeant A.H. "Strawb" McEgan poses. (A.H. McEgan via David Vincent)

The original artwork for "Barhootee the Cootee" drawn up by Bob McMahon prior to his transfer to the 33rd Pursuit Squadron (Provisional). (Robert F. McMahon)

Flying trainee Cadet Elton S. Perry during his training with Class 41-F at Stockton Field California during 1941. Perry was the first shot down over Darwin on February 19, 1942. (NARA via Shane Johnston)

Cootee No II"/ "MAC," but it fared no better and was damaged in a landing accident on February 18, much to the displeasure of Pell who threatened to have McMahon convert to B-18s and fly in fuel supplies when the unit reached Timor. With considerable effort McMahon and his mechanics managed to get a third aircraft serviceable, though electrical problems and an intermittent radio persisted. Pell's aircraft, tail number "3," also had problems. On the morning of the planned flight to Timor it was unserviceable with a Prestone coolant leak. Pell commandeered Lt. Robert H. Vaught's "28" and ordered the young lieutenant back to Brisbane to join up with another unit. Pell's aircraft was towed to the 12 Squadron hangar for repairs.

With his remaining aircraft, Pell eventually took off for Timor at 0915hrs, escorted by a 19th Bombardment Group B-17 navigation aircraft, 41-2417, *San Antonio Rose II*, flown by Lt. Clarence L. McPherson. Only a few minutes into the flight, deteriorating weather, including a 600-foot ceiling and heavy rain, was reported over Timor by the RAAF Meteorological Officer at Koepang. Pell was faced with the decision whether to continue or return to

Darwin and, based on the advice of both the USAAF operations officer at Darwin, Captain Louis J. Connelly, and 19th Bombardment Group pilot, Lt. Hewitt "Shorty" Wheless – and no doubt fully aware of the inexperience of his pilots, Pell turned back while the B-17 flew on.

Pell and his brood were back over Darwin at 0934hrs, even as Father McGrath at the Bathurst Island Mission was preparing to transmit a message reporting a large formation of aircraft overhead to Lou Curnock at the coastal radio station in Darwin. Pell and his "A" Flight descended to land at the RAAF Station leaving five to remain on patrol under the command of the "B" Flight leader, Lt. Jack Peres. With him were Lieutenants Oestreicher, Elton Perry, William Walker and Max Wiecks.

THE STRIKE FORCE LAUNCHED

By the early hours of Thursday February 19, 1942, VAdm. Nagumo's carriers were at a prearranged launch point some 220 miles northwest of Darwin. A weather reconnaissance aircraft had been launched from the cruiser *Tone* at dawn and arrived over Darwin at around 0730hrs Darwin time. Despite being able to receive, the aircraft's radio was unserviceable and no report was received aboard the *Akagi*. With the weather fine and clear, Nagumo ordered the strike.

Since before dawn the mechanics had been arming the aircraft, running engines and systems, topping up fuel tanks and carrying out last-minute checks. The pilots and crews had been briefed by Capt. Minoru Genda and Cdr. Mitsuo Fuchida, the attack leader.

The pilots and crews of the aircraft were briefed on their roles. From the *Akagi* the Kates were to bomb the harbour facilities and shipping, the Vals were to dive-bomb and strafe shipping while the Zekes were to intercept any Allied fighters and strafe targets of opportunity. For the Kates on the *Kaga*, their targets were military installations including Naval HQ, government buildings and the main jetty; the Vals were to attack shipping, the Darwin Civil 'Drome and the RAAF Station, while the Zekes were to intercept any Allied fighters and strafe targets of opportunity. The *Hiryu* Kates were assigned the role of those of the *Kaga*, its Vals were to attack shipping and the Zekes were to conduct the same role as those of the *Akagi* and *Kaga*. For *Soryu*, its Kates were to bomb shipping and military installations, the Vals were to attack shipping and military installations, while the Zekes were assigned what was no doubt the disappointing role of top cover for the attack force. The pilots of 15 Zekes assigned in five rotating *shotai* as a Combat Air Patrol (CAP) over the carriers would have been even more disappointed.

By 0615hrs Tokyo time the carriers were in position to launch aircraft and the order was given soon after. First off seven minutes later was Fuchida from the flagship *Akagi*, followed by 17 of his Kates. Eighteen Kates under Lt. Heijiro Abe followed from *Soryu* four minutes later and a further 18 from *Hiryu* under Lt. Cdr. Tadashi Kosumi took off at 0628hrs. They were followed at 0655hrs by 27 Kates from *Kaga*, led by Lt. Cdr. Takashi Hashiguchi. The Zekes followed: nine aircraft (a *chutai* comprising three *shotai* of three aircraft) each from the *Soryu* and *Hiryu* led by Sub Lt. Iyozo Fujita and Lt. Sumio Nono. Last off were the Vals and their escorts: 18 each

Inward tracks of the Japanese attacking forces, February 19, 1942.

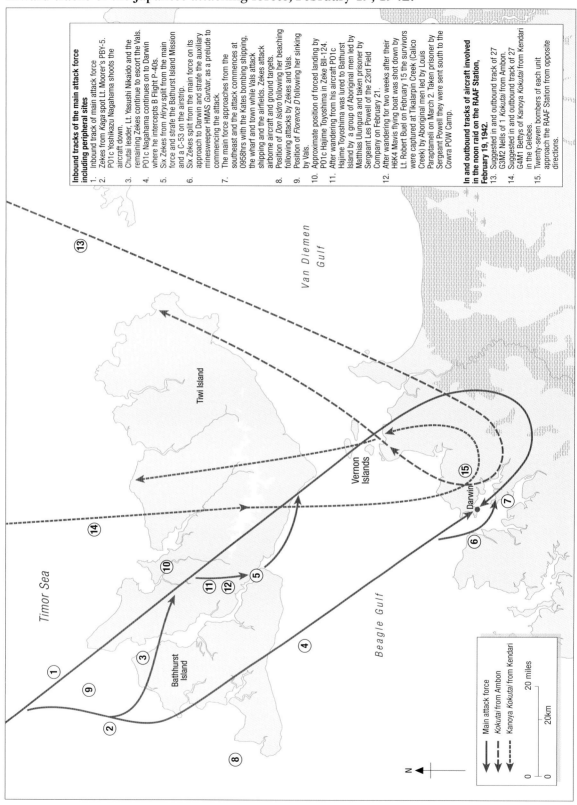

Inbound tracks of the main attack force including peripheral sites

1. Inbound track of main attack force
2. Zekes from *Kaga* spot Lt. Moorer's PBY-5. PO1c Yoshikazu Nagahama shoots the aircraft down.
3. Chutai leader, Lt. Yasushi Nikaido and the remaining Zekes continue to escort the Vals. PO1c Nagahama continues on to Darwin where he intercepts B Flight P-40s.
4. Six Zekes from *Hiryu* split from the main force and strafe the Bathurst Island Mission and a C-53 on the airstrip.
5. Six Zekes split from the main force on its approach to Darwin and strafe the auxiliary minesweeper HMAS *Gunbar*, as a prelude to commencing the attack.
6. The main force approaches from the southeast and the attack commences at 0958hrs with the Kates bombing shipping, the wharf and town while Vals attack shipping and the airfields. Zekes attack airborne aircraft and ground targets.
7. Position of *Don Isidro* following her beaching following attacks by Zekes and Vals.
8. Position of *Florence D* following her sinking by Vals.
9. Approximate position of forced landing by PO1c Hajime Toyoshima in Zeke BII-124.
10. After wandering from his aircraft PO1c Hajime Toyoshima was lured to Bathurst Island by a group of Aboriginal men led by Matthias Ulungura and taken prisoner by Sergeant Les Powell of the 23rd Field Company on February 21.
11. After wandering for two weeks after their H6K4 Mavis flying boat was shot down by Lt. Robert Buel on February 15 the survivors were captured at Tikalarpin Creek (Calico Creek) by Aboriginal men led by Louis Paraptameli on March 2. Taken prisoner by Sergeant Powell they were sent south to the Cowra POW Camp.

In and outbound tracks of aircraft involved in the noon raid on the RAAF Station, February 19, 1942.

13. Suggested in and outbound track of 27 G3M2 Nells of 1 *Kokutai* from Ambon.
14. Suggested in and outbound track of 27 G4M1 Bettys of Kanoya *Kokutai* from Kendari in the Celebes.
15. Twenty-seven bombers of each unit approach the RAAF Station from opposite directions.

Van Diemen Gulf

Tiwi Island

Vernon Islands

Darwin

Bathurst Island

Timor Sea

Beagle Gulf

Main attack force
Kokutai from Ambon
Kanoya *Kokutai* from Kendari

0   20 miles
0   20km

N

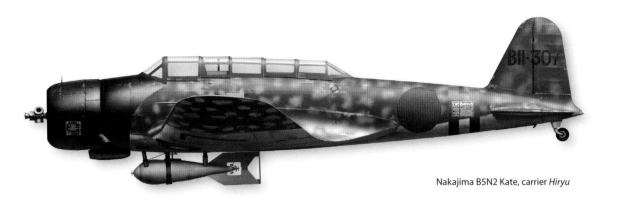

Nakajima B5N2 Kate, carrier *Hiryu*

from *Akagi*, *Kaga* and *Soryu* under Lts. Takehiko Chihaya and Shoichi Ogawa, and Lt. Cdr. Takashige Egusa respectively. Only 17 Vals under Lt. Michio Kobayashi launched from *Hiryu*, while nine Zekes each from *Kaga* and *Akagi* led by Lt. Yasushi Nikaido and Lt. Cdr. Shigeru Itaya completed the attack force of 188 aircraft. All but Fujita and Kobayashi had participated in the Pearl Harbor raids.

At 0700hrs Fuchida and his crew of pilot, Lt. Mitsuo Matsuzaki, and radio operator and rear gunner, Flight PO1c Tokushin Mizuki, passed over the convoy and set a course of 148 degrees for Darwin.

At much the same time the force of 54 land-based bombers was preparing to depart bases at Ambon and Kendari to follow up the attacks by the carrier-borne force. Twenty-seven Betty bombers of Kanoya *Ku* of the 21st *Koku Sentai* at Kendari were to be led by Lt. Cdr. Toshiie Irisa while Lt. Cdr. Takeo Ozaki was to lead his 27 Nells of 1 *Ku* from Ambon. The Bettys departed at 0635hrs Tokyo time, followed five minutes later by the Nells and, after joining up, headed for Darwin.

Bound for Darwin one of nine Zekes launches from VAdm. Nagumo's flagship *Akagi* while Val dive-bombers line up at rear.

FIRST VICTIMS

Admiral (at the time) Thomas H. Moorer photographed in 1967. From his exploits of February 1942 he went on to become Chairman of the Joint Chiefs of Staff before retiring in 1974.

By 0915hrs Darwin time, the aerial attack fleet had spread out over the Tiwi Islands comprising Melville and Bathurst Islands when the westernmost element, the *chutai* of *Kaga*-based Zekes, spotted a lone aircraft flying some miles away from a surface vessel, later identified as the Filipino-registered blockade runner, *Florence D*. The aircraft, a Consolidated PBY-5 Catalina coded 22-P-9 (previously 22-P-4), was to become the first casualty of the day. Flown by Lt. Thomas H. Moorer and crew, the aircraft, Bu No. 2306, on strength to Squadron VP-22 of Patrol Wing (PatWing) 10, had cleared the northwestern tip of Bathurst Island when she was spotted.

While eight of the fighters, including *chutai* leader Lt. Yasushi Nikaido, looked on briefly before heading off to escort their Vals, PO1c Yoshikazu Nagahama, the second pilot in the 3rd *Shotai*, peeled off and attacked the lumbering flying boat. A 1938 graduate of *Ko* 2 Flight Trainee Course at Yokosuka *Kokutai*, the experienced Flyer1c Yoshikazu Nagahama had flown as No. 2 to PO1c Kiyonobu Suzuki over Pearl Harbor and had participated in the Wake Island raid.

Thomas Moorer and his co-pilot, Ensign Walter H. Mosley, had taken off from Darwin harbor at 0800hrs. As Moorer later reported:

> [We] headed on a northerly course to conduct a routine patrol in the vicinity of Ambon … an unreported merchantman was observed off the north cape of Melville Island… When about ten miles from the ship I was suddenly attacked by nine fighters… At the time I was proceeding down wind at 600 ft.

Nagahama's attack with 20mm cannon and 7.7mm machine guns set "my plane afire, destroying [the] port engine and putting large holes in [the] fuel tanks and fuselage," Moorer wrote:

> I endeavoured to turn into the wind but all fabric except starboard aileron was destroyed and it was discovered that with one engine and all fabric missing

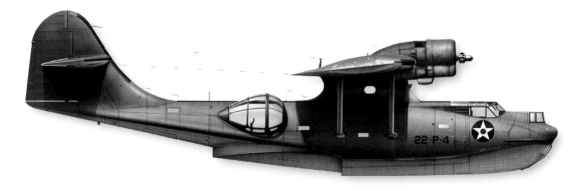

PBY-5 Catalina of VP 22, Patrol Wing (PatWing) 10, 22-P-4 (22-P-9). Lt. Thomas L. Moorer

from port side an indicated speed of 110 knots was necessary … to keep the plane straight and level. There was no alternative but to land … and this was rendered even more hazardous [in] that the float mechanism had been destroyed by gunfire… At this time I glanced back and observed large streams of fuel pouring from both tanks and the fire extending along port side. Small balls of fire were bouncing around and noise created by bullets striking the plane was terrific.

Assisted by a badly wounded Mosley, Moorer managed to get the aircraft down:

[striking] the water at a great force but after bouncing three times managed to complete the landing… The port waist gun was untenable due to extreme heat but LeBaron … manned the starboard gun and vigorously returned the enemy fire… One boat was discovered to be completely full of holes but [a second] boat was launched through the navigator's hatch. By this time the entire plane aft of the wings was melting and large areas of burning gasoline surrounded the plane.

The second casualty of the day was a Douglas C-53, a version of the DC3, C-47 series, No. 41-20051 of the USAAF's 22nd Transport Squadron sitting on the Bathurst Island Mission airstrip awaiting repairs. As the attack fleet flew across the Tiwi Islands the Sacred Heart Catholic Mission was attacked, along with the stranded C-53, when six Zekes from *Hiryu* split from the main force and strafed the mission buildings and airstrip. The aircraft was destroyed and a number of buildings including the radio shack were damaged, the latter possibly to prevent any messages from being transmitted and silence any warning of the Japanese force, in contrast to the widely held belief that the radio had been jammed by the Japanese.

Douglas C-53, No. 41-20051 of the 22nd Transport Group was strafed on the Bathurst Island airstrip by Zekes from *Hiryu*. It was pushed off the cliff in the postwar years. (AWM, Negative 152203)

They were too late. Alerted to the large force of aircraft by the Tiwi people at the mission, Father John McGrath had hurried to the radio shack and called Darwin on frequency 6840. There he made contact with Lou Curnock, the duty operator at the Amalgamated Wireless Australasia (AWA) coastal radio station under the call sign VID. Curnock logged McGrath's message: "0935 hours 8SE [Bathurst Island call sign] to V.I.D. Huge flight of planes passed overhead bound Darwin." "Roger," Curnock replied, "Roger, stand by." Curnock then reported the message to RAAF Operations at 0937hrs, logging it as "phoned to RAAF" and tried to re-establish contact with McGrath, however the mission

©Jim Laurier

LT. THOMAS MOORER AND PBY-5, 22-P-4 (PP. 44–45)

Lieutenant Thomas H. Moorer and his co-pilot, Ensign Walter H. Mosley, had taken off from Darwin harbor in Consolidated PBY-5 Catalina Bu No. 2306 at 0800hrs on the morning of February 19, 1942 on a patrol mission in the vicinity of Ambon. A second Catalina aircraft of the US Navy's Patrol Wing (PatWing) 10 flown by Lt. Robert "Buzz" Le Fever was to patrol the area around Timor. Rounding the northwestern tip of Bathurst Island and shortly after spotting the Filipino blockade runner, the *Florence D*, Moorer's Catalina flying boat was spotted by nine Zekes from the carrier *Kaga*. One Zeke flown by PO1c Yoshikazu Nagahama (**1**) split from the group and attacked Moorer's aircraft, setting it on fire and severely damaging it, while the remaining eight aircraft led by Lt. Yasushi Nikaido flew on towards Darwin. With his aircraft on fire and no option but to attempt to alight, Moorer set the aircraft down. After a hazardous landing at speed and with only

one wing tip float extended, Moorer and his crew managed to exit the badly damaged aircraft (**2**) while a crewman T.R. Le Baron continued firing on the attacking Japanese fighter (**3**) before rejoining the crew. Rescued later that morning by the second of the blockade runners *Don Isidro*, which was subsequently sunk by dive-bombers, they were taken on board the *Florence D*. The Japanese attacked and sank the *Florence D* off Melville Island that afternoon with one of Moorer's crewmen, Aviation Machinist's Mate 2c, J. C. Schuler, killed in the attack. Moorer and his remaining crew took charge of the group of survivors in two lifeboats and drifted onto Bathurst Island some hours later. Although they were first spotted by a RAAF Hudson it was a further day before a RAAF Wirraway dropped supplies and water. They were rescued by the Australian Navy's HMAS *Warrnambool* on February 21 and returned to Darwin.

was off the air after McGrath had hastily abandoned the shack as the Zekes from *Hiryu* strafed the mission and the USAAF C-53 at the airstrip. The Darwin RAAF operations officer, Flt. Lt. A. Saxton, called the RAAF Station Commander, Wg. Cdr. de B. Griffith, to the Operations Room, noting the time the message was received as between 0940 and 0945hrs. Saxton informed Griffith that the message had been sent to both Combined HQ and HQ North-West Area but, despite Griffith's concern that the aircraft might not have been friendly, nothing more was done.

INITIAL COMBAT

The apparent confusion over the aircraft reported by Father McGrath was later suggested to have been due to the unexpected return of the ten P-40Es of Pell's 33rd Pursuit Squadron (Provisional). Despite the main force having been reported but not yet over Darwin, one Japanese aircraft, that of PO1c Yoshikazu Nagahama, had been noticed some minutes before, reportedly between 0937 and 0945hrs.

The first over the target after downing Moorer's PBY-5, Nagahama had flown on alone, arriving over Darwin at 0937hrs even as Pell led four of his P-40s to land at the RAAF Station and leaving "B" Flight to patrol over Darwin. According to the *Kaga* operations report, the *Kodochosho*, Nagahama, "Spotted two enemy small planes (P-40s), jointly attacked the two planes and shot them down (one of them uncertain). Continued to fly, spotted two enemy small planes (P-40s) … [and] shot down the two planes."

The first warning of enemy aircraft came when, according to Oestreicher, he and his flight had climbed through 8,000ft when he "spotted a ship diving on the formation from about two thousand feet above us and in the eight o'clock position. Upon recognizing him I radioed 'Zeros, Zeros, Zeros.'" The initial attack broke up the formation and two of the Americans, Lts. Elton S. Perry and Max Wiecks, were shot down in quick succession, though Oestreicher maintained in his subsequent report that Peres was the first to be downed. According to Bob McMahon, however, Peres landed at the RAAF Station, apparently leaving Oestreicher to lead the patrol.

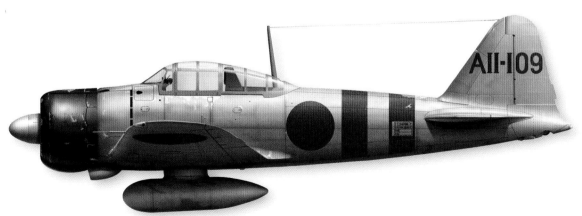

Mitsubishi A6M2b Type O fighter, carrier *Kaga*. PO1c Yoshikazu Nagahama

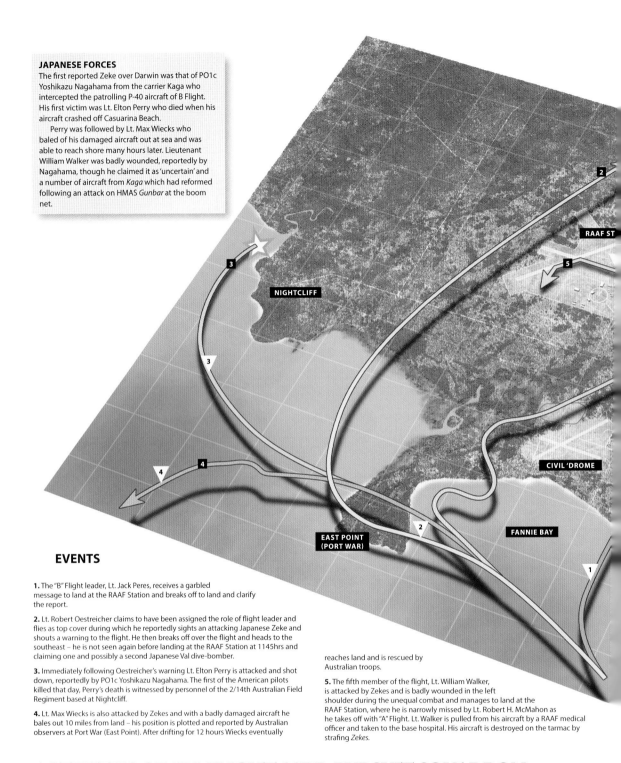

JAPANESE FORCES
The first reported Zeke over Darwin was that of PO1c Yoshikazu Nagahama from the carrier *Kaga* who intercepted the patrolling P-40 aircraft of B Flight. His first victim was Lt. Elton Perry who died when his aircraft crashed off Casuarina Beach.

Perry was followed by Lt. Max Wiecks who baled of his damaged aircraft out at sea and was able to reach shore many hours later. Lieutenant William Walker was badly wounded, reportedly by Nagahama, though he claimed it as 'uncertain' and a number of aircraft from *Kaga* which had reformed following an attack on HMAS *Gunbar* at the boom net.

RAAF ST

NIGHTCLIFF

CIVIL 'DROME

FANNIE BAY

EAST POINT
(PORT WAR)

EVENTS

1. The "B" Flight leader, Lt. Jack Peres, receives a garbled message to land at the RAAF Station and breaks off to land and clarify the report.

2. Lt. Robert Oestreicher claims to have been assigned the role of flight leader and flies as top cover during which he reportedly sights an attacking Japanese Zeke and shouts a warning to the flight. He then breaks off over the flight and heads to the southeast – he is not seen again before landing at the RAAF Station at 1145hrs and claiming one and possibly a second Japanese Val dive-bomber.

3. Immediately following Oestreicher's warning Lt. Elton Perry is attacked and shot down, reportedly by PO1c Yoshikazu Nagahama. The first of the American pilots killed that day, Perry's death is witnessed by personnel of the 2/14th Australian Field Regiment based at Nightcliff.

4. Lt. Max Wiecks is also attacked by Zekes and with a badly damaged aircraft he bales out 10 miles from land – his position is plotted and reported by Australian observers at Port War (East Point). After drifting for 12 hours Wiecks eventually

reaches land and is rescued by Australian troops.

5. The fifth member of the flight, Lt. William Walker, is attacked by Zekes and is badly wounded in the left shoulder during the unequal combat and manages to land at the RAAF Station, where he is narrowly missed by Lt. Robert H. McMahon as he takes off with "A" Flight. Lt. Walker is pulled from his aircraft by a RAAF medical officer and taken to the base hospital. His aircraft is destroyed on the tarmac by strafing *Zekes*.

ACTIVITIES OF "B" FLIGHT 33RD PURSUIT SQUADRON (PROVISIONAL), FEBRUARY 19, 1942

As the Japanese attack force approaches Darwin from the southeast, five P-40 fighters of "B" Flight 33rd Pursuit Squadron (Provisional) USAAF are left to patrol over Darwin by the unit Commanding Officer, Maj. Floyd Pell. Leading "A" Flight, Pell lands at the RAAF Station after having to abort a planned flight to Koepang, Timor, due to bad weather en route.

Note: Gridlines are shown at intervals of 1km

ALLIED FORCES

The only aircraft available to the Allies on February 19, 1942 were ten Curtiss-Wright P-40E Warhawks (Kittyhawks to the Australians) of the 33rd Pursuit Squadron (Provisional) USAAF under the command of Maj. Floyd Pell. The presence of the ten aircraft was fortuitous as they had been forced to return to Darwin following the report of bad weather en route and at their intended staging point at Koepang on Timor.

Five aircraft of "B" Flight were left to maintain a patrol over Darwin but were quickly overcome by attacking Japanese fighters. One remained in the air and returned to the RAAF Station some time after the Japanese had returned to the carriers.

1. Lt. Jack Peres
2. Lt. Robert Oestreicher
3. Lt. Elton Perry
4. Lt. Max Wiecks
5. Lt. William Walker

DARWIN TOWN

Nagahama reportedly downed Perry, the first airman killed in combat over Darwin, followed by Wiecks, and Walker. Perry's death was witnessed by personnel of the 2/14th Australian Field Regiment at Nightcliff, when at "approx 0950 hrs" unit observers reported "Enemy planes & our own fighters seen in dogfight off Nightcliff … the first plane to be shot down, a US Kittyhawk, was observed by members of the Regiment, but it took some time to convince Headquarters … that the event had occurred."

Wiecks baled out some 10 miles out to sea after his aircraft had been damaged in combat. Going into a flat spin, he recalled, "Nothing I did corrected [it] and as I was close to the water I knew I had to jump. I jettisoned the canopy and unbuckled my seat belt. Immediately I was catapulted out of the cockpit and had just opened my parachute when I heard the thud of the plane as it hit the sea." Supported by a semi-inflated Mae West, he alternately swam and floated during the day, while battling Darwin's 20-foot tides. Noticing the shore was getting closer as darkness fell he finally reached it "just as the moon was going down." Moonset that night was at 2205hrs; he had spent over 12 hours in the water. "I saw a tree in front of me," he recalled, "I was exhausted but had enough strength to grab it and strap myself to it. I stayed there all night. At dawn I was able to walk to the sand. I went along a track to an Australian camp and was taken to hospital."

Walker was luckier. Badly wounded in the left shoulder during the one-sided combat, he was able to land his aircraft but was narrowly missed by McMahon as he "scrambled" with Pell's "A" Flight. "I took off just over Walker as he was rolling off the North runway intersection," McMahon recalled, "and I was directly under a flight of six [Zekes] (in two elements of three) who were in combat echelon about 200–300 ft. above me (probably planning to peel off on Walker, then taxiing)."

Walker taxied to the 13 Squadron hangar apron, where he was assisted from his aircraft and taken to the RAAF Station hospital. A report, *Darwin Air Raids – 19th February 1942*, detailed: "Whilst the Japanese were still strafing and bombing the R.A.A.F. Station, Flt. Lt. Horan, a medical officer, prevented a patient, Flt. Lt. Jenkins, from going to the aid of one of the American Kittyhawk pilots, and proceeded himself into the open to the injured man's aid and took him to the hospital for treatment. [Horan] Then assisted him to the shelter trench as the raid progressed."

Walker's aircraft was strafed and burnt shortly afterwards as Lt. Vaught had prepared to take it into combat – wisely he took advice and sheltered in a nearby slit trench. In just a few minutes two pilots were dead and another badly wounded, three aircraft were lost and Oestreicher had flown off towards Batchelor. It was then up to Pell and his flight.

A RAAF fitter walks towards Lt. Bill Walker's P-40E on the 13 Squadron tarmac. Lieutenant Vaught was to take it off but wisely opted to shelter in a nearby slit trench – it was destroyed moments later. (A.H. McEgan via David Vincent)

THE STRIKE FORCE APPROACHES

As the main Japanese attack force crossed the Tiwi Islands. PO1c Takeyoshi Morinaga, the observer in the lead Kate aircraft of the 3rd *Shotai*, 3rd *Chutai* off the *Kaga*, recalled seeing "tropical trees like coconut palm trees," as his aircraft passed over Melville Island, "and I believe I saw crocodiles near a river." The Japanese aircraft would also have been seen and heard as the attack force crossed the north coast of Bathurst Island, by a small bedraggled group of Japanese aircrew who must have watched them in some confusion. The group consisted of survivors of the Mavis flying boat downed by Lt. Buel four days prior.

Once past the Tiwi Islands the Japanese attack force flew over Clarence Strait and the Vernon Islands before crossing the coast north of Oscar and Evan Herbert's Koolpinyah Station east of Darwin at 0945hrs. Fuchida's force turned to the west and then northwest over the 27-mile peg at Noonamah on the run in to Darwin. At 0955hrs the formation approached the target from the southeast and still no alarm had been sounded in Darwin. Three minutes later the first enemy bombs detonated on Australian soil.

While the alarm had not sounded in Darwin itself, the Japanese had been spotted and fired upon by the 3.7-inch antiaircraft guns of both 2 and 14 HAA Batteries. 2 HAA Battery based at Berrimah, east of Darwin, reported sighting the enemy formations at 0950hrs and firing 60 rounds, while the War Diary of 14 HAA Battery reported, the "Alarm [was] sounded 0950 hours squadrons of Japanese bombers sighted approaching from south at great height approx. 15000 ft. All sections immediately went into action and engaged aircraft."

Even as the formations approached unscathed by the AA fire, they had been preceded by Zekes, Takeyoshi Morinaga recalled. Thirty-six Zekes had escorted the Kates and Vals but the 27 remaining after the *Kaga* Zekes had separated on spotting Moorer's PBY, split from the main strike force just before its arrival to commence a preliminary attack. Six Zekes swept in at 0957hrs and strafed the auxiliary minesweeper, HMAS *Gunbar*, as it passed through the harbor boom gate, wounding nine, including the skipper, Lt. N.M. Muzzell, who received bullet wounds to both legs. Another, Ordinary Seaman H.J. Shepherd, died aboard the hospital ship *Manunda* two days later and was buried at sea.

Darwin town, the wharf area and harbour viewed from the west in early 1942. The attacking Japanese force approached from the southeast after turning north over the 27-mile peg, Noonamah.

Attack patterns of the Japanese aircraft, February 19, 1942.

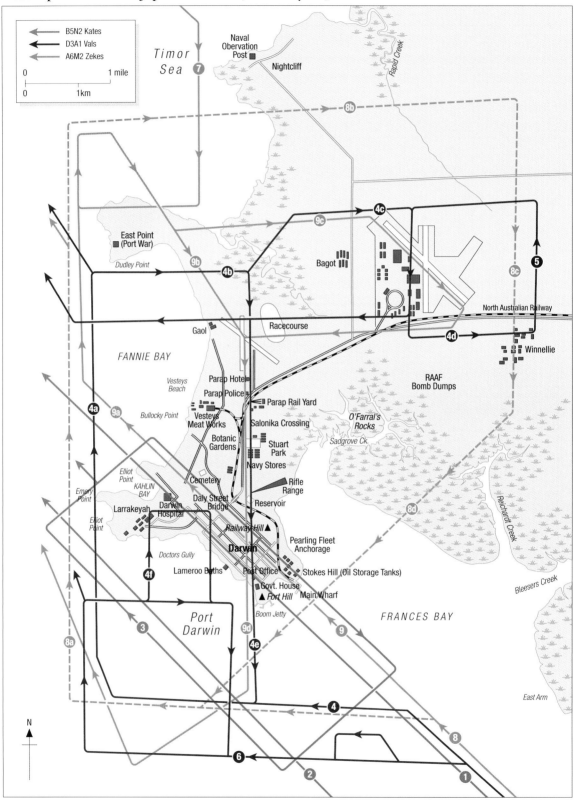

B5N2 Kates

1. Direction of approach and exit for return to the carriers of the B5N2 Kates of *Kaga* while bombing the main wharf and government buildings (Government House, Post Office, Military Barracks, homes and the Darwin Hospital). Each of the 81 Kates carries an 800kg bomb.
2. Direction of approach and exit for return to the carriers of the B5N2 Kates from *Akagi*, *Hiryu* and *Soryu*, while bombing the harbour and shipping.
3. The attack force leader, Cdr. Mitsuo Fuchida, remains overhead to monitor the attack. Following the attack he photographs the results and returns to the carrier *Akagi*.

D3A1 Vals

4. The D3A1 Vals of the carrier *Kaga* carry out bombing and strafing attacks on the shipping, the Civil 'Drome and the RAAF Station. Each of the 71 Vals carries a 250kg bomb.
5. The location of D3A1 Val No. 3304 in which FCPO Katsuyoshi Tsuru and his pilot, Flyer1c Takezo Uchikado, were killed when their aircraft crashed at Ironstone Knob after being hit by ground fire from the Winnellie camp.

6. The D3A1 Vals of *Akagi*, *Hiryu* and *Soryu* attack shipping in the harbour, while those of the *Soryu* are tasked to attack a number of military sites before exiting to return to the carriers.

A6M2 Zekes

7. After downing a Catalina off Bathurst Island, PO1c Yoshikazu Nagahama flies on to Darwin where he intercepts the P-40s of "B" Flight 33rd Pursuit Squadron (Provisional) USAAF before rejoining his flight. Lieutenant Elton Perry is attacked and shot down, reportedly by Nagahama. The death of Perry, the first of the American pilots killed that day, is witnessed by personnel of the 2/14th Australian Field Regiment based at Nightcliff. Nagahama is credited with four aircraft destroyed during the raids.
8. The nine A6M2 Zekes of the carrier provide top cover for the main attacking force (8a to 8d show their suggested patrol perimeter).
9. The remaining Zekes of *Akagi*, *Kaga* and *Hiryu* carry out their assigned task of intercepting any Allied aircraft and strafing targets of opportunity including the Civil 'Drome, the RAAF Station, Darwin town and shipping on the harbour. (9a to 9d show their suggested tracks though this is much simplified).

THE AERODROMES

Peter Roberts, a gunner at East Point, also witnessed the attacks and in particular those by the Zekes on the nearby Civil 'Drome:

> We were used to watching … the Americans playing tag … dog fighting… Next thing there was splash … then a second splash. Then we realised it was more than just fooling. Then a rumble of bombs … in the city itself [and] on the harbour… We knew it was on! But, by the time we were in our trenches the Zeros were overhead … we started firing at the aircraft with .303s. Ten Zeros … followed up … strafing the civil 'drome … they seemed to fly in a circuit, coming from the civil 'drome down East Point … bank … drop down over Dudley Point and go in low to attack. It was absolutely to a pattern … at only 150 to 200 feet when they banked over us.

Some of 12 Squadron's Wirraways were dispersed under cover at the Civil 'Drome when the Japanese first struck. Bruce Beales, an observer with the squadron, recalled how he and his pilot were walking towards their aircraft and both "looked up to see three aircraft zooming around … we thought they were Americans … suddenly we realised they were firing at each other. We … then broke into a run as 'Val' dive bombers proceeded to strafe and then bomb… Fortunately they did not find our [camouflaged] aircraft." The aerodrome, hangar and infrastructure were badly damaged and remained unused until repairs were effected later that year.

Elsewhere, on the RAAF Station, at the Winnellie and Parap camps, at Berrimah, on the oil tanks overlooking the harbor, on ships and scattered throughout the area, small-arms fire also targeted the Japanese aircraft as they made their bombing and strafing runs. Among a number of light machine-gun posts at the RAAF Station, one, a .303-inch Vickers G.O. (Gas Operated) gun mount was manned by the area armament officer, Wg. Cdr. Archibald Tindal, who had served as a pilot with No. 24 Squadron at Rabaul before being posted to Darwin in January 1942.

Damage to the Qantas/Guinea Airways hangar and buildings at the Civil 'Drome was extensive after it was attacked by Vals and Zekes. The camouflaged Wirraways of No. 12 Squadron escaped unscathed.

David Hopton, a pilot with No. 12 Squadron, recalled, "Early in February '42 Wing Commander Archie Tindal started digging a round hole six feet deep … this served to tell us that the Japanese were coming. [He] said he was building a frame to hold 2 Vickers gas operated machine guns. The hole was only 50 feet from our hangar." On the morning of February 19, Tindal manned the machine gun when the raid began. He was firing when a round from a strafing aircraft struck him in the throat and killed him. Tindal was one of eight airmen, one an American flight engineer, killed on the RAAF Station during the two raids.

The attacks on the RAAF Station saw one and possibly two Japanese aircraft lost. One, a Val "dive bomber was seen approaching from the R.A.A.F. some time after the general bombing started. As it approached Sappers Fred Terrone and Dick Spedding with the Lewis gun started firing at it. The rest of

Australian Army personnel inspect the wreckage of Aichi D3A1 Val No. 3304 following its being shot down over Winnellie camp. (John Watts Collection, NT Library)

the Detachment fired their rifles," the War Diary of 1/54 Anti-Aircraft Searchlight Company recorded. "Suddenly there were cries of 'We got it etc' [sic] and the plane was seen to belch smoke and the pilot and rear gunner slump in their cockpits. The plane dropped its nose and some seconds after it disappeared from our view, we heard a terrific crash and explosion. I rang Headquarters at McMillans and reported the claim to Lt. George Patterson ... [who] came out to Ironstone later that day and the incident described and the claim for a hit was again made by the Detachment personnel."

Both crew members were killed in the crash and buried in a makeshift grave nearby. Gunner Des Lambert recalled that two days later, on:

The pilot and observer of Val No. 3304 were buried in a bush grave near the wreckage of their aircraft. The inscription on the marker reads "Unknown Japanese Airmen Died 19.2.42" (Ron Wattus)

> Saturday, 21st February, I received permission from Maj. Nigel Sutherlan[d], O.C. of 2nd A.A. Battery to search for the wreckage which fell in the bush a mile or so from Berrimah. Accompanied by Bombardier James Glennie I walked along the railway line for some distance then headed towards the bush on the other side of the line. We came across some ambulance drivers camped near a gravel road: they directed us to the crash site. The wreckage was in a hole and parts of one or two of the crew buried nearby. A soldier was busy with a hacksaw trying to remove the three-bladed propellor. Borrowing a machete, I hacked off part of a wing tip as the O.C. wanted a trophy for the orderly room. An officer arrived, driving an [sic] utility truck, and drove us back to Berrimah with the large "trophy". I decided to leave the pilot's helmet on the fuselage, which became a mecca for many souvenir hunters, until there was little left.

Another young Japanese pilot, PO1c Hajime Toyoshima also struck trouble over Darwin when small-arms fire holed the oil tank of his Zeke over the Parap Camp. He got as far as Melville Island before his oil tank bled dry and his propeller sheared off. He force landed and after some days was captured by young Aboriginal men.

A SQUADRON DECIMATED

As the Japanese struck, Pell attempted to lead his flight into the air, despite some difficulty in releasing his drop tank before it was cleared from beneath the aircraft by his crew chief, Sergeant Roy Bopp. After taking off from the north–south runway, Pell flew low to the north with Zekes following. Avoiding some Zekes, Bob McMahon "saw a P.40 [sic] racing around to my left, banked and headed back in [the] direction of the hangars. I started to join up with him but saw a chute stream out from the plane (this was evidently Pell) so I reversed my direction."

Pell was attacked by Zekes and killed near King Creek at Camerons Beach northeast of the RAAF Station after parachuting from his aircraft at only 80 feet. According to a number of authors he was strafed and killed by

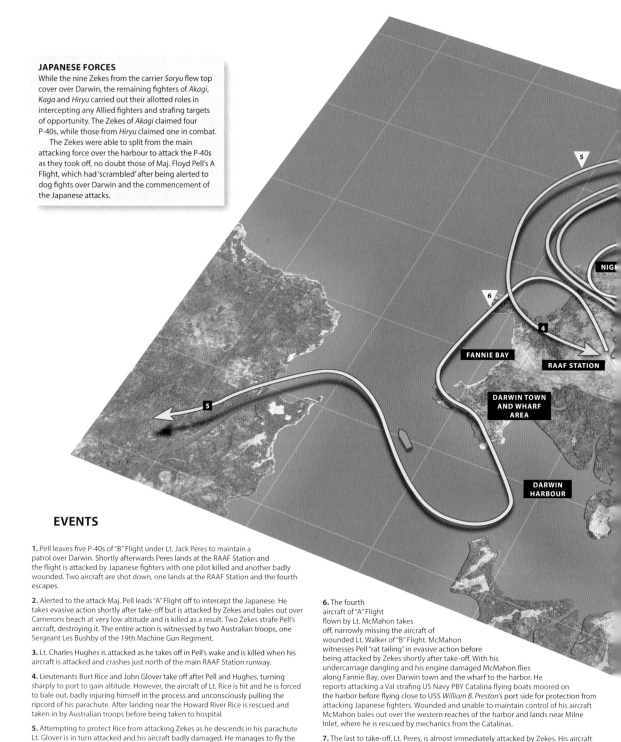

5

NIG

6

4

FANNIE BAY

RAAF STATION

5

DARWIN TOWN AND WHARF AREA

DARWIN HARBOUR

EVENTS

1. Pell leaves five P-40s of "B" Flight under Lt. Jack Peres to maintain a patrol over Darwin. Shortly afterwards Peres lands at the RAAF Station and the flight is attacked by Japanese fighters with one pilot killed and another badly wounded. Two aircraft are shot down, one lands at the RAAF Station and the fourth escapes.

2. Alerted to the attack Maj. Pell leads "A" Flight off to intercept the Japanese. He takes evasive action shortly after take-off but is attacked by Zekes and bales out over Camerons beach at very low altitude and is killed as a result. Two Zekes strafe Pell's aircraft, destroying it. The entire action is witnessed by two Australian troops, one Sergeant Les Bushby of the 19th Machine Gun Regiment.

3. Lt. Charles Hughes is attacked as he takes off in Pell's wake and is killed when his aircraft is attacked and crashes just north of the main RAAF Station runway.

4. Lieutenants Burt Rice and John Glover take off after Pell and Hughes, turning sharply to port to gain altitude. However, the aircraft of Lt. Rice is hit and he is forced to bale out, badly injuring himself in the process and unconsciously pulling the ripcord of his parachute. After landing near the Howard River Rice is rescued and taken in by Australian troops before being taken to hospital.

5. Attempting to protect Rice from attacking Zekes as he descends in his parachute Lt. Glover is in turn attacked and his aircraft badly damaged. He manages to fly the aircraft to the RAAF Station where he crash lands and is badly injured – he is pulled from the aircraft and transported to hospital where he undergoes facial surgery.

6. The fourth aircraft of "A" Flight flown by Lt. McMahon takes off, narrowly missing the aircraft of wounded Lt. Walker of "B" Flight. McMahon witnesses Pell "rat tailing" in evasive action before being attacked by Zekes shortly after take-off. With his undercarriage dangling and his engine damaged McMahon flies along Fannie Bay, over Darwin town and the wharf to the harbor. He reports attacking a Val strafing US Navy PBY Catalina flying boats moored on the harbor before flying close to USS *William B. Preston*'s port side for protection from attacking Japanese fighters. Wounded and unable to maintain control of his aircraft McMahon bales out over the western reaches of the harbor and lands near Milne Inlet, where he is rescued by mechanics from the Catalinas.

7. The last to take-off, Lt. Peres, is almost immediately attacked by Zekes. His aircraft crashes inland from Hope Inlet and it is not until September 1942 that it is located and his remains are identified by an inscribed Bulova watch.

ACTIVITIES OF "A" FLIGHT 33RD PURSUIT SQUADRON (PROVISIONAL), FEBRUARY 19, 1942

As the Japanese attack force approaches Darwin from the southeast, five P-40 fighters of "A" Flight 33rd Pursuit Squadron (Provisional) USAAF, led by the unit Commanding Officer, Maj. Floyd Pell, land at the RAAF Station after having to abort a planned flight to Koepang due to bad weather en route.

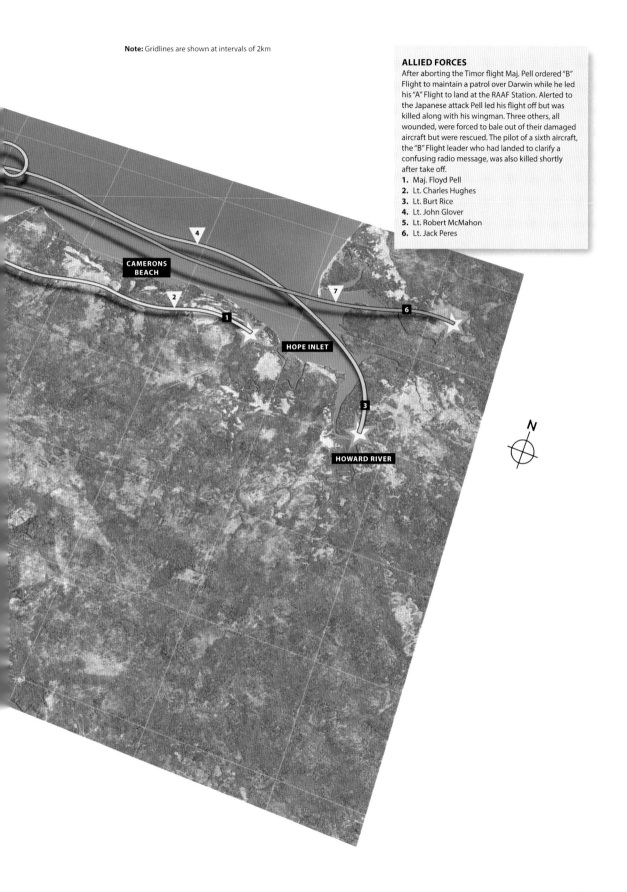

Note: Gridlines are shown at intervals of 2km

ALLIED FORCES

After aborting the Timor flight Maj. Pell ordered "B" Flight to maintain a patrol over Darwin while he led his "A" Flight to land at the RAAF Station. Alerted to the Japanese attack Pell led his flight off but was killed along with his wingman. Three others, all wounded, were forced to bale out of their damaged aircraft but were rescued. The pilot of a sixth aircraft, the "B" Flight leader who had landed to clarify a confusing radio message, was also killed shortly after take off.

1. Maj. Floyd Pell
2. Lt. Charles Hughes
3. Lt. Burt Rice
4. Lt. John Glover
5. Lt. Robert McMahon
6. Lt. Jack Peres

CAMERONS BEACH

HOPE INLET

HOWARD RIVER

Australian Army personnel at the crash site of Maj. Floyd Pell's P-40 on the desolate mud flats of Camerons Beach. Pell's body was recovered and identified by Lt. McMahon later that day. (Shane Johnston)

Zekes as he attempted to crawl away: a contention that has been disproved by two Australian Army witnesses to the incident. One, Sergeant Les Bushby of the 19th Machine Gun Regiment, was at Camerons Beach and recalled looking up to see:

two aeroplanes well up in the air on top of one very low down [we] saw one come down heard shots then saw the one underneath turn around and come down about 20 yards from me and dive into the mud the pilot left the plane and came into the mud 15 foot short of the plane. Planes wings were off I ran over to him rifle loaded held out in front of me, the Jap plane came down fired into the plane in mud and it exploded, lifted me into the air landed face full of mud 10 foot away from him. I ran away the other plane fired 14 explosive bullets at me as I ran about 50 yards. I went back to the pilot his parachute had opened as he came down laid out and his heart wasn't beating the plane that had shot him down flew over me about 20 foot up... I took a book out of the Pilots shirt pocket [and it read] Captain Floyd James Pell.

Closely following Pell, Lt. Charles Hughes was killed by attacking Zekes from *Hiryu*, which reported downing an aircraft on takeoff. Even before he gained enough flight speed and altitude Hughes crashed immediately north of the RAAF 'Drome, while McMahon, Peres, Burt Rice and John Glover succeeded in becoming airborne but were immediately attacked by enemy fighters.

Peres' death was not witnessed by any of the other pilots, though it is known that he was shot down and killed shortly after takeoff, his aircraft crashing near Tree Point at Hope Inlet northeast of Darwin. The circumstances surrounding Peres supposedly having been the first to fall and his position subordinate to Oestreicher in "B" Flight have been written about by a number of authors, apparently based entirely on a July 1942 report by Oestreicher. The report, when related to other information, is inconsistent and contradictory, as are his retrospective logbook and diary. Recollections of events recorded in his July 1942 report on the activities of the 33rd Pursuit Squadron (Provisional), which over the years have become "conventional wisdom," have also been disproved, including his contention that Peres was the first American pilot killed that day. His stated appointment by Pell as "B" Flight leader has also come into question.

As the appointed "B" Flight leader, Peres had apparently handed over to Oestreicher while he returned to the RAAF Station, possibly with an unserviceable aircraft, but as Bob McMahon recalled, his radio was intermittent and while he could not confirm it:

in our (Sunday morning Q. back session at Berrimah) [a meeting of the surviving pilots was held at 119 Australian General Hospital at Berrimah on February 20, 1942] it was brought out that (apparently immediately after Pell told the flight to go to 15,000) an unidentified and a rather garbled call or 2 calls came for all the P40's [sic] at Darwin to return to the field and land. Evidently Peres didn't recognize the voice (We did ID pretty much by voice recognition and there was no mistaking Pell's). Jack Peres apparently asked for a repeat of the recall and was questioning it, when the tower who had better receivers than the P40 then repeated the call saying all P40's are instructed to return and land! The tower thereby added a recognizable voice to obviously conflicting instructions and further confused the situation. It is my opinion that about this juncture, Peres might have told Ostericher [sic] to watch the flight as Perry, Walker and Weike [sic] were relatively low on flight experience. This could [also] have been the basis for Ostericher's claiming to have been a flight leader – however, nobody in Htrs. [sic] ever heard of leading a flight from weaving above it!

McMahon further recalled that after landing he was:

writing up the plane's faults [when] a crewman ran out and yelled the Japs are here! Then back to his slit trench! I called him back and asked him how he knew … at that time a Bren Gun carrier ½ track came up with Peres on it. He jumped off and ran toward me pointing up (his chute on). I nodded, started up. He jumped back on the carrier and rattled off in the dust. – So I know he wasn't shot down on the first pass (as reported – and neither was I).

Second Lieutenant Charles Hughes poses in front of the family home in Hamilton Ohio following his graduation from flying training at Kelly Field, San Antonio, Texas in late 1941. (Gordon Birkett)

Peres' aircraft and remains were reported by local Aboriginal people on September 5 that year. Peres was still in his aircraft, identified only by his engraved watch. Clyde H. Barnett, a P-40 pilot with the 8th Squadron 49th Fighter Group, remembered:

Capt. Sims came around a couple of times and once when he was here, Capt. Powell, old G-10 came by and he would meet Sims, Sims to be flying [sic] up east of Darwin where they had found the wreck of a P-40 and a skeleton. He came back later in the day with the remains of a Bulova watch, in pretty good shape. It had the name "Jack Peres" engraved on its back. [Lt.] Dockstader said he was here in that Feb. 19 raid and he was probably shot down then.

Following takeoff and sighting Pell's imminent demise, Bob McMahon reversed his direction:

by about 45° and at that time a Zero caught up with me and his burst dropped my gear – it was impossible then to outrun them but somehow I lasted another

©Jim Laurier

THE DEATH OF MAJOR PELL (PP. 61–62)

At 0915hrs February 19, 1942 Maj. Floyd Pell led his nine Curtiss Wright P-40 Kittyhawks from the Darwin RAAF Station en route to Timor. Forced back by a severe weather front at Koepang and on the advice of his escorting B-17 aircraft – and no doubt with the inexperience of his pilots in mind – Pell led his squadron, the 33rd Pursuit Squadron (Provisional) back to the RAAF Station. Once over Darwin he left five aircraft of "B" Flight to patrol while he led his "A" Flight down to refuel before relieving them on patrol. In the meantime PO1c Yoshikazu Nagahama had flown on after downing Lt. Thomas H. Moorer's Catalina off Bathurst Island; arriving over Darwin ahead of the main force he attacked "B" Flight, downing two of the P-40s, killing one pilot and wounding the pilot of a third aircraft. The main attack then commenced at 0958hrs and, alerted to the raid, Pell led "A" Flight off to combat

the Japanese four minutes later. His wingman, Lt. Charles Hughes, was killed on take-off and Pell was attacked soon after. Taking immediate evasive action he was set upon by the Zekes (**1**) and in trying to escape his attackers, he flew at low level away from the RAAF Station to the north and east, witnessed by one of his flight, Lt. Robert F. McMahon. With his aircraft badly damaged Pell baled out; however he was too low for his parachute to fully open and was killed when he hit the ground (**2**). The action was observed by Australian Sergeant Les Bushby and a fellow Australian Army private (**3**), who ran towards Pell's body, narrowly escaping a strafing Japanese attacker. Removed to the mortuary at 119 Australian General Hospital that afternoon, Pell was later identified by Lt. McMahon when he was admitted with wounds received in combat.

15–16 minutes… My survival was probably due more to the fact that they were like fish in a feeding frenzy and damn near running into one another… I got several good shots into at best between 3 and 5 enemy aircraft and at least three of them seem to have been vitally hit. My total time start up to out of parachute was about 26–28 minutes of which about 18–19 minutes was pure dog fight.

McMahon ranged from the airfield across the northern coastline to the west, then "rat tailed" south across town, down to the wharves, past an unidentified ship, cut around the Australian hospital ship *Manunda* and back across the harbor before heading northwest then west and finally baling out and landing in the mangroves of Woods Inlet.

McMahon was the only pilot to bale out over the harbour that day and the unidentified ship he passed was undoubtedly the USS *William B. Preston*. Lieutenant Herb Kriloff was on the bridge of the vessel when "A P-40 fighter was spotted ahead, flying low and trailing smoke. Stone shouted, 'Cease fire,' but in this melee that was impossible. The P-40 swung low, running down our port side, with the apparent hope that we take the Japanese fighters off his tail. We were successful in doing this, but after passing us he pulled up and bailed out."

Despite his aircraft having been shot up, possibly by Nagahama and his *shotai*, and his undercarriage slowing him McMahon was able to stay in the air long enough to attack a Japanese two-seat aircraft strafing three US Navy PatWing 10 Catalinas before having to bale out of his burning P-40. He parachuted to safety and was picked up in a creek on the western side of Darwin harbour by some mechanics of the US Navy's PatWing 10. He was fortunate.

The mechanics had been working on one of the three PBY Catalinas, 22-P-41, moored on the harbour when they were strafed by Zekes, one of them Nagahama, according to the *Kaga Kodochosho*, and possibly from the carriers *Akagi* or *Hiryu*. The US Navy mechanics, Ed Aeschliman, Tom Anderson and Herb Casey rapidly abandoned the burning aircraft in a life raft but were strafed and became separated. Aeschliman made it to a line of mangroves and watched a P-40 pilot bale out and parachute into mangroves. In the meantime Casey was experiencing difficulties and was rescued by Anderson before they were all picked up by a whaleboat from USS *Preston*. Aeschliman reported seeing the P-40 pilot and that he had been strafed in his parachute on the way down. They located McMahon, still in his parachute, hanging from a tree. Wounded and unable to release himself,

A US Navy Consolidated PBY-4 Catalina of PatWing 10 at its moorings on Darwin harbor in 1941. In all, four Catalinas of PatWing 10 were destroyed on February 19, 1942.

the three sailors cut him down and he was taken to 119 AGH at Berrimah where he later identified Pell's remains.

McMahon later recalled his plight after his:

> 'chute opened at about seven hundred feet. I heard a rat-tat-tat behind me and a plane going by. They were shooting at me… I began climbing up the 'chute-riser. The Japanese shot out some shroud lines but I got down into mangroves… It was quiet there after all the noise… I didn't know which way to go. I was lost… I climbed a tree and could see nothing and thought I'd die there. My boots were full of blood and mud. I had no emergency kit. But I had a compress on my belt and I bandaged my leg with that. I saw that I wasn't far from the sea. I waded out, sat on my rubber parachute seat, and flailed the water to frighten any crocodiles. The current took me across the mouth of a stream. From there I could see a motor boat … and I started yelling. They must have cut the motor because they heard me and came to take me off.

Flying trainee Cadet John G. Glover during his training with Class 41-G at Kelly Field, Texas, 1941. Recovering from his ordeal on February 19, 1942, he served in the Pacific and European Theatres before retiring as a colonel. (NARA via Shane Johnston)

KF (7.15-41)A/C GLOVER, JOHN G.

Lieutenants Burt Rice and John Glover were last off according to Douglas Lockwood in his book *Australia's Pearl Harbour* [sic], though they would have preceded Peres, who had to return to his aircraft, strap in, start up and taxi after speaking with McMahon. McMahon supports this in stating that an aircraft he encountered north of the airfield when no Zekes were in sight, "could only have been Peres. He had to be last off!"

Rice was in trouble almost immediately after taking off when he and Glover turned sharply to port and began climbing while also attempting to evade attacking Zekes. Rice had barely reached 5,000 feet and was about to turn into a Zeke when he found his controls had been shot away and were not responding. With his aircraft entering a flat spin he baled out, striking his head with such force on the way that he was blinded and lost consciousness. He landed safely in swampy country on the eastern side of the Howard River in Shoal Bay and was taken in by troops of the Australian 19th Machine Gun Regiment under Lt. Tom Shelton, but could not recall pulling the ripcord.

From Shoal Bay, Rice was taken to 119 AGH at Berrimah later that day, for treatment to his wounds, though, according to the *Reno Evening Gazette*, he was unsure when they were inflicted, "whether in the dog-fighting or after he bailed out he does not know for certain – 'so I just tied my arm to my neck and started walking.'" Despite his admittance to 119 AGH the same day, he was reported in his hometown newspaper the *Reno Evening Gazette* as having been in the mangroves for five days with "an aching thirst and hunger relieved only by a couple of salt-water-soaked chocolate bars."

Rice was fortunate to have survived and would not have, had it not been for the action of "A" Flight's No. 5, John Glover. "While Rice swung helplessly in his parachute the Japanese became aware of his predicament. They circled him … and began coming

Positions of aircraft crash sites, Darwin, February 19, 1942

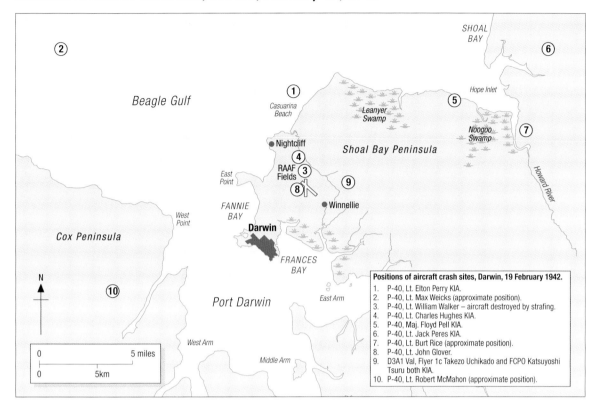

Positions of aircraft crash sites, Darwin, 19 February 1942.
1. P-40, Lt. Elton Perry KIA.
2. P-40, Lt. Max Weicks (approximate position).
3. P-40, Lt. William Walker – aircraft destroyed by strafing.
4. P-40, Lt. Charles Hughes KIA.
5. P-40, Maj. Floyd Pell KIA.
6. P-40, Lt. Jack Peres KIA.
7. P-40, Lt. Burt Rice (approximate position).
8. P-40, Lt. John Glover.
9. D3A1 Val, Flyer 1c Takezo Uchikado and FCPO Katsuyoshi Tsuru both KIA.
10. P-40, Lt. Robert McMahon (approximate position).

at him with machineguns blazing… Glover had the luck to find one of the Zeros chasing Rice directly in his gunsight. He pressed the button and saw it going down," Douglas Lockwood wrote:

> Then he saw the Zeros circling Rice and using him as an Aunt Sally. Glover abandoned his climb for altitude to break them up in what observers in the trenches on the aerodrome below regarded as a valiant but suicidal act. Glover began orbiting Rice's parachute in tight circles in an attempt to protect him at three thousand feet his plane, critically damaged, went into a steep dive… Men watching him were convinced, when he did not bail out that Glover

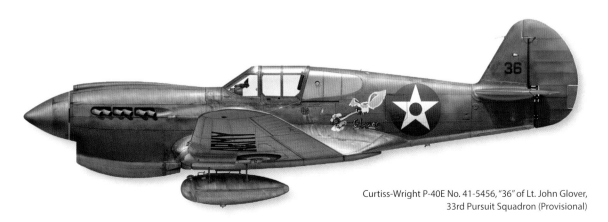

Curtiss-Wright P-40E No. 41-5456, "36" of Lt. John Glover, 33rd Pursuit Squadron (Provisional)

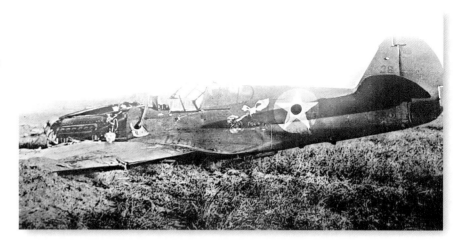

himself had been hit. He had, however, been struggling to regain control. At the last instant … the P.40 [sic] levelled off, hit the edge of the aerodrome, cart-wheeled several times in clouds of dust and smoke and smashed into pieces that flew for one hundred yards from what remained of the fuselage.

At 119 AGH the following day Glover related to Bob McMahon that "I got one of the little son's of bitches [sic] – just blew him up then they got me… I was diving away from two of them, leveled out and looked back and they seemed to be closing up, so I put the stick and throttle forward and I was in the … trees."

With the wings all but torn from it, Glover's aircraft finally came to a stop. Those who witnessed the incident were sure that the pilot could not have survived. However, a badly injured and shocked Glover managed to exit the wreckage and walk a few paces before sitting down and burying his head in his hands. With the threat of strafing Japanese aircraft and Glover's exposed position a quick-thinking Australian airman rushed from his slit trench and dragged the dazed pilot to safety. Told later that Glover had been rescued by two Australians, McMahon commented, "I don't know if they were ever awarded but it was one of the bravest acts performed by the ground personnel that day."

The injured Glover, his face swathed in bloodied bandages, was taken to 119 AGH, where he was admitted by Matron Edith McQuade White. Glover was placed in a ward and the bandages removed, revealing, according to McQuade White, "a gaping wound extending through forehead to nose and chin. Haemorrhage was profuse." In shock, Glover rambled, telling of his shooting down a Japanese aircraft and agitating over the loss of two watches he had been wearing. It was 2200hrs before he could be operated on by Maj. Coles and his surgical staff; it was almost dawn when they finished. Matron McQuade White also found one of Glover's watches with the personal effects she had been handed on his admission and the other was returned by a chaplain, who had found it near Glover's aircraft.

Through it all Glover not only had his two watches returned but he had retained his bloodied Mae West. When he was evacuated aboard the hospital ship *Manunda*, Glover gave the Mae West to Maj. George Whitely of the 148th Field Artillery Regiment who had been aboard the vessel *Portmar* and badly wounded. As Whitely reportedly had a liking for collecting items that represented important events on his life, "Lt. Glover gave it to him as it was just a piece of government issue [sic] that would be replaced but to Major Whitley [sic] it was a memento of what happened to him on Feb 19th 1942. Both he and Glover were rather in poor shape." Glover survived with only a faint scar to remind him of his combat. The Mae West is now displayed at Darwin's East Point museum facility.

Of the four American pilots killed, two remain unaccounted for. Perry has yet to be located, though identifiable components of a Curtiss P-40 have been recovered from Casuarina Beach near Nungalinya or Old Man Rock, including a gun bay cover and an undercarriage leg. Parts of what were suspected to have been Hughes' aircraft were found during roadworks in Darwin's northern suburbs in the mid-1960s, though his remains have yet to be located. The 33rd Pursuit Squadron (Provisional) was no more, though one pilot and his aircraft survived the day's events unscathed.

THE ENIGMATIC LIEUTENANT OESTREICHER

Oestreicher had remained in the air for two and a half hours before landing at 1145hrs, claiming one Val shot down and a second that he had seen smoking, after reportedly intercepting them.

In his combat report of July 21, 1942 Oestreicher reported:

After receiving orders from Major Pell to take my flight to fifteen thousand feet I started to climb. At eight thousand feet I spotted a ship diving on the formation from about two thousand feet above us and in the eight o'clock position. Upon recognising him I radiod [sic] "Zeros, Zeros, Zeros." On his first attack he broke our formation and forced us to dive out dropping belly tanks at the same time. Climbing back into the sun I was able to get a small burst into one Zero who rolled in his climb and shot me. I spun out regaining control around four thousand feet. I again climbed and around twelve thousand feet I countered [sic] eighteen more planes in a lazy circle at what I would judge to be twenty thousand feet. I called up "B" Flight on the radio and advised heading for the clouds about five miles south of Darwin that were at an altitude of about two thousand feet to twenty-five hundred feet. After flying among the clouds for about half an hour I spotted two Series 97 dive bombers with fixed landing gear on a course heading for Batchelor Field. Intercepting them at about fifteen hundred feet I fired and saw one definitely burst into flames and go down. The other was smoking slightly as he headed for the clouds. I lost him in the clouds. At approximately 11:45 I landed at the RAAF Field with my left tire [sic] and wheel shot up. Service and armament crews immediately began to service the ship. Private Ceech and Private Bujold began to hunt for a wheel and tire I could use on my plane. Private Lindquist an excellent armorer, [sic] reloaded my guns. I went to Twelve Squadron Hangar and there reported to Captain Whela as [sic] and General Patrick Hurley what had happened and I thought I had shot down one plane and that the other might be classed as a "probable." The following morning I took off at dawn and flew to Daly Waters where a Squadron Leader Connely [sic] took charge of repairing my plane. Later that same afternoon a report came through that a coastal artillery battery had located both planes within a mile of each other. These were the first confirmed aerial victories on Australian soil. On February 27, I received telegraphic orders to fly south and report to the 49th Pursuit Group at Bankstown, N.S.W.

While Oestreicher reported firing on one Zeke after releasing his drop tank and joining the combat, that and his subsequent actions came under critical scrutiny the following day when four of the surviving pilots discussed the events at 119 AGH. When McMahon asked how the flight got bounced, both Walker and Wiecks agreed:

> that the other driver's [Oestreicher's] actions (or lack of) contributed to it, as they were circling to the Left headed North East to North. Oestreicher peeled off over them, headed to the South East in about a 40° dive – they were wondering what was wrong with him – when his belly tank came off and about 3 seconds later called "Zeros" but didn't give any direction – They thought at first he was diving on some but actually he dove directly away from the attacking Zeros and when the rest of the Flight looked around they all had Zeros on their ass!! [sic] … and according to Walker when last seen, Oestreicher was heading directly for the cloud cover at Batchelor … and was not seen in the fight again.

Tellingly, Oestreicher did not visit the hospital facility to enquire after his fellow pilots later in the day, though he may have been placed on alert in expectation of further raids. It seems also either that word may either have gotten back to him regarding the critique or that McMahon spoke with him when they later encountered each other in Brisbane, as his retrospective diary intimates, "Hughes, Perry and Peres all killed in combat. McMahon, despite what he blows on about was shot down on T.O. and did not shoot down any Japs. He too as well as the rest of the boys all received the D.S.C. and now mine is supposed to be coming thru."

Oestreicher went on to claim the two Vals, and, in a letter to his father, he wrote of the day's events, "The entire story I cannot tell you. Suffice it to say that I have two Nip notches on my belt." In the event he was awarded one victory. However even this cannot be substantiated. Oestreicher's actions and his claims that day have come under further scrutiny in the number of contradictions and inconsistencies in his subsequent reporting of the events, including his meeting up with Brig. Gen. Hurley, his retrospective logbook and diary (both were lost in an aircraft accident in October 1942 and reconstructed), interviews and correspondence. He has in effect become somewhat of an enigma and with it his July 1942 report has become suspect.

Oestreicher left Darwin at dawn and flew to Daly Waters on February 20, according to his report of July 21, 1942. However, this is countered by his own admission that on that same day he went to the wreckage of the Val and came away with a piston, which was later fashioned into an ashtray. Bob McMahon also recalled:

> Between 12 & 1 p.m. on 20 Feb. Capt. Shorty Wheeler [sic] was driving me … to Batchelor Field Hospital. We stopped at the field and there was his, Bob Ostericher's [sic] P.40. I recognized it because of its markings [a sharkmouth and the name "Miss Nadine"]. We were parked about 30ft from the plane and my leg wouldn't let me get out and inspect it. But a staff Sgt. came up and saluted. I inquired as to the status [of the aircraft] and the Sgt. stated that he had personally checked and preflighted that plane and that it was ready to go, armed etc. but they were unable to find the pilot.

THE NOON RAID

As ordered, but in the light of the results of the carrier force attack probably unnecessary, the morning raid was followed up with a noon raid on the RAAF Station by 27 Bettys of a detachment of Kanoya *Kokutai* at the newly acquired base at Kendari in the Celebes and 27 Nells of 1 *Ku* from Ambon. The 27 Betty bombers of Kanoya *Kokutai* of the 21st *Koku Sentai* at Kendari were led by Lt. Cdr. Toshiie Irisa while Lt. Cdr. Takeo Ozaki led his 27 Nells of 1 *Kokutai* from Ambon. The Bettys departed at 0635hrs Tokyo time, followed five minutes later by the Nells and, after joining up over the Banda Sea, headed for Darwin.

Taken from the waist gunner's position, a *chutai* of G3M2 Nells is pictured on its way to a target. Twenty-seven of the type released 318 60kg bombs in the noon raid on the RAAF Station.

Each of the Bettys was armed with 60kg bombs totaling 212 for the force plus one 250kg bomb, while the Nells were armed with a total of 318 60kg bombs.

As the combined bomber force flew towards Darwin, a Babs of 3 *Kokutai* overflew Darwin to photograph and report on damage caused by the carrier-borne force. The unit action report, the *Kodochosho*, recorded, "The land reconnaissance plane reconnoitered Port Darwin at 1010 [Tokyo time]."

As the bomber force approached Darwin the two units separated, with 27 aircraft flying in from different directions before releasing their loads. Ken Tinkler, an RAAF electrician, recalled, "Power was restored just in time to activate the Air Raid Alarm for the second raid, when two flights of aircraft appeared, one heading ... north east to south west and the other south east

Devastation in the 12 Squadron hangar. Two P-40s are in foreground, with A-24 41-15794 at centre. A Wirraway, A20-180, is at left. It was later written off. (A.H. McEgan via David Vincent)

to north west." An official RAAF report on the raids recorded, "A formation of 27 aircraft in line abreast (followed by) another flying in a head-on direction to the first." The result of this pattern bombing was widespread destruction and damage to the RAAF Station. Murry Lawson, an RAAF Fitter with No. 2 Squadron, recalled seeing "two flights of 27 [aircraft] each which pattern bombed the aerodrome. I heard bomb bursts getting closer and closer – then they finally stopped."

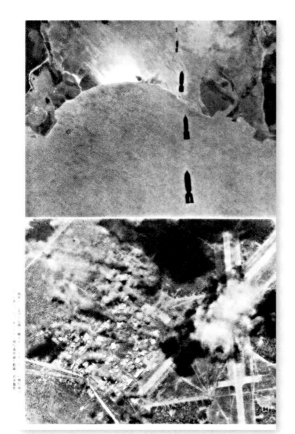

Two images produced in a wartime Japanese book show at top, 60kg bombs released over Nightcliff foreshore and below, their impact on the RAAF Station.

Suffering no losses and leaving the RAAF Station devastated, the Japanese aircraft departed the area unhindered but for some slight shrapnel damage from the A-A fire and landed back at their bases at 1530hrs and 1435hrs (Tokyo time) respectively.

The report of the raid by the Japanese was brief:

The 27 land-based attack-planes from the Kanoya Air Group as well as the 27 land-based attack-planes from the 1st Air Group air-raided Port Darwin; they bombed the eastern airport [RAAF Station] at 1037 and 1040 (respectively) ... all the bombs hit the airport facilities and the runway, causing big fires in a large hanger [sic] and two small hangers [sic] in the south and facilities in the adjacent area (a large hanger [sic] in the north had already been on fire) [i.e. the 12 Squadron hangar], setting two large planes on fire, and inflicting serious damage on one medium-sized plane, and four small planes, and ... one of [the Japanese aircraft] received gunshot damage.

ATTACKS ON THE *DON ISIDRO* AND *FLORENCE D*

Following the morning raid and a run over the harbor to observe results, Fuchida signalled for the return of his force to the carriers at 1050hrs Darwin time, though some had departed earlier, including the *chutai* of Zekes from the *Soryu*. As top cover for the attacking force they had seen no action and would have been keen to become involved. As they flew northwest across the Tiwi Islands to the coast, they spotted a vessel steaming north of Cape Fourcroy on the northwestern side of Bathurst Island.

Led by Sub Lt. Iyozo Fujita, the Zekes attacked the ship, strafing it with cannon and machine-gun fire, reporting, "While taking duty to directly protect the attack force, strafed one armed merchant cruiser to slow its speed." The captain of the vessel, the Filipino-registered USAT *Don Isidro*, was more descriptive. In his report of February 21, the ship's master, Rafael Cisneros, wrote:

At about 9.15 a.m. [Manila time – 1045hrs Darwin time] seven fighting planes were sighted, and came to machine gun us savagely. In spite of all efforts done by the crew to avoid such punishment, and the nice behavior performed by Lt. Kane and his detail of gunners to giving them back the same fight, we were hit severely destroying all our life boats and life rafts, and causing a good number of holes on every side of the ship, besides the injuries received by several members of the crew. This happened at about 25 miles off North Bathurst Island.

The *Don Isidro* had been spotted earlier, however, when an aircraft returning from Darwin to *Akagi* had reported it as a 6,000-ton-class armed merchant cruiser 100 nautical miles north of Port Darwin. Vice Admiral Nagumo immediately ordered the cruisers *Tone* and *Chikuma* to make contact with the vessel, while ordering *Soryu* and *Hiryu* to attack it. *Tone* launched an Aichi E13A1 Jake floatplane, which located *Don Isidro* "at about 1.30 p.m. [1500hrs Darwin time] [when] a bomber was sighted and dropped us two [60kg] bombs which were lucky again not to be hit," Cisneros reported.

In the meantime, Thomas Moorer and his crew had managed to clear the crash site of their PBY-5 and "After rowing for about thirty minutes we were picked up by *Florence D*, flying an American flag but with a Filipino crew," Moorer later reported. The *Florence D* was the vessel Moorer had spotted prior to the attack on his aircraft and had witnessed the distant action. "Shortly afterwards" Moorer continued, "Japanese planes were sighted returning from Darwin. An S O S was intercepted from *Don Isidro*, about twenty miles to our north, stating that she was under continuous attack and afire with many wounded ... while we were going to her aid, a twin-float seaplane approached and dropped two bombs near us. We were then strafed by machinegun fire."

At much the same time, crews were refueling and arming nine Vals on each of the carriers *Soryu* and *Hiryu* with a single 250kg bomb each. The *chutai* leaders, Lieutenants Masai Ikeda and Michiji Yamashita, were to mount attacks on the vessel previously spotted by the returning aircraft from *Kaga* and subsequently strafed by the Zekes, the *Don Isidro*.

Aided by the E13A1 Jake from *Tone*, the Vals from *Soryu* found the *Don Isidro* steaming at 18 knots on a course of 200°, 30 nautical miles north of Cape Fourcroy, and began the attack at 1456hrs Tokyo time. "[T]he attack force bombed and strafed this enemy about ten nautical miles away at 0 degrees from Cape Fourcroy," the Japanese reported. "Three 250 kilo bombs hit the ship leaving it unable to navigate."

For the crew on board *Don Isidro*, it meant further punishment and further injuries. Rafael Cisneros reported "a bunch of nine or perhaps more of dive bombers and several fighter planes [sic] attacked and bombed us in every corner savagely and severely and consequently the ship was in complete flames... I decided to beach the ship heading East, which we were not able to do, as the engines stopped instantly, and we were about three miles off [Cape Fourcroy] then, but the attack continued until they saw the whole ship burning disastrously and completely disable[d]."

With *Don Isidro* severely damaged and dead in the water, Cisneros and his remaining crew, including Lt. Kane and his US Army gunners, abandoned the vessel and struck out for land. Even as they did, the Vals from *Hiryu* had located the second vessel, *Florence D*, "32 nautical miles and 350 degrees from Cape Fourcroy," and attacked her. From his vantage point aboard *Florence D* Thomas Moorer reported, "carrier-type dive-bombers were seen going towards *Don Isidro*." Some 30 minutes later he:

The wreck of the US Army's Philippines blockade runner, *Don Isidro*, lies beached and abandoned off Bathurst Island. She is protected under the Commonwealth Historic Shipwrecks Act 1976, as is the *Florence D* further north.

heard the whine of a dive-bomber and was knocked down by a terrific explosion in the bow, followed by the explosion of ammunition. A second bomb hit us amidships... I groped my way aft amid the burnt and wounded and ordered my crew over the side... *Florence D* was well down by the bow [but] the attack continued. Three bombs missed the ship and burst near us. We suffered terrible pain in the testicles, stomach, back and chest, and coughed and spat blood. I fear Schuler [a US Navy crewman aboard the PBY-5] was killed in this way, for a bomb was seen to explode very close to him.

Their mission accomplished, the Vals flew off to their respective carriers, which then retired to Staring Bay in the Celebes for replenishment and further forays into the NEI, the Pacific and the Indian Oceans.

With the *Florence D*'s Master, Carmelo Manzano, badly wounded and three other Filipino crewmen killed, Moorer took command and ordered the survivors into two lifeboats. After floating on driftwood for an hour, he was picked up by one of the lifeboats and assumed command of it and 23 survivors, while, despite his wounds, his co-pilot Ensign Mosley took over the other with 17 aboard. After a voyage of around nine hours the survivors made landfall on the western side of Bathurst Island, having been directed towards land by an RAAF Hudson of No. 2 Squadron, which had spotted the survivors in the water on the late afternoon of the 19th. However, as the second pilot, Flying Officer H.S. "Jim" McDouall, recalled, "We couldn't do much to help them but give them a friendly wave and point them in the direction of land." From there they attempted to walk across the island to the Catholic Mission but, in light of the number of injuries, were forced to abandon the attempt and await rescue.

The survivors from *Don Isidro* also reached the western side of Bathurst Island, though some hours after those from the *Florence D*. Cisneros reported:

We figured it was about 2.00 or 3.00 o'clock in the morning ... and we have been beached separately. Then we joined and checked each other and found that four were dead and many were missing. Part of the crew endeavoured to locate the others until the relief vessel H.M.A.S. "Warrnambool" came to [us] about 10.30 a.m. on February 20th, 1942 and [we] found that part of the missing crew were picked up by the same boat at different points on the island. Once we were on board ... we found seven missing besides the four dead.

The survivors were taken to Darwin where they were accommodated overnight at the Darwin Hospital at Kahlin before being taken to the US Army's 147th Field Artillery Regiment camp at the 16-mile peg opposite the Howard Springs turnoff south of Darwin, prior to being evacuated to Brisbane.

On Bathurst Island the *Florence D* survivors had a further day to wait before rescue. The morning after the *Don Isidro* survivors had been picked up, a "R.A.A.F. [Wirraway] aircraft spotted our boats and by writing in the sand we identified ourselves and asked for food, water and medicine. We had been without food for 48 hours," Moorer reported, "The plane returned later and dropped supplies. We were picked up on 22 February by H.M.A.S. *Warrnambool*, in command of Lieut E.J. Barron R.A.N.R. We were attacked by a Japanese flying boat while going aboard but *Warrnambool* laid a smoke screen and cleverly manoeuvred [sic] to avoid being hit."

AFTERMATH

JAPANESE LOSSES

As Fuchida's force returned to the carriers, aircraft were inspected for damage as the pilots and crews reported their actions and verbally submitted claims. Damage was relatively light with a majority of the aircraft suffering hits by small-arms fire and some shrapnel damage from bursting AA rounds. Two Vals, one the last in the 1st *Chutai* and the other the second last in the 3rd *Chutai*, both from *Kaga*, were forced to land with their 250kg bombs hung up after unsuccessfully attempting to jettison them. Both made it safely, no doubt to the relief of all concerned.

In a later report the damage was detailed as the number of hits by individual projectiles:

Carrier	Zekes	Kates	Vals
Akagi	3 hits	0 hits	1 hit
Kaga	4 hits	7 hits	6 hits 1 self-destruction
Soryu	0 hits	4 hits	10 hits
Hiryu	7 hits 1 self-destruction	4 hits	2 hits
Totals	14 hits plus 1 self-destruction	15 hits	19 hits plus 1 self-destruction

Note. The term "self-destruction" was used to denote the loss of an aircraft in action and in most cases reflected that the crew had died heroically by sacrificing themselves by crashing into targets. In this case they were reported to have "voluntarily crashed into the target with the crew dying heroic deaths."

While all the reports made by the flyers on their return to the carriers have yet to be translated, a number have recalled their roles in more recent years, though none mentions any aircraft lost in the raid. Takeyoshi Morinaga, who had described the trees and crocodiles as they flew over the Tiwi Islands, related, "I was carrying an 800kg bomb, just like at Pearl Harbor; I was told to drop it on military headquarters and government buildings. I picked a building, dropped the bomb and I saw a huge explosion. After the sand and smoke disappeared I saw nothing on the ground. The building had disappeared."

Another, Sadao Yamamoto, an observer aboard a Kate from the *Hiryu* recalled that while he could not identify the building he bombed, "From the air I could just make out a huge, white and round shaped structure. I judged it to be one of the military barracks they had told us were in that area... I could see the damage to [it]. About two thirds of it had turned black when we flew back over." A Kate pilot from the *Kaga*, Takeshi Maeda, related to journalist Matthew Franklin his role in the Pearl Harbor raid and "After that I'm sorry to say I had to attack Darwin... It was a simple mission. I dropped bombs and then I went home." Maeda was more forthcoming with author Ron Werneth on his part in the Darwin raid, recalling:

> My Type 97 *kanko* [Kate] was armed with one 800 kilogram bomb. This was the first time I saw Australia, which had deep green foliage and peaceful blue water... Inside the harbor were enemy destroyers, but they had become the prey for our Type 99 *kanbaku* [Val], so our Type 97s had no target to attack. I saw a hospital ship but we couldn't attack it ... our commander had no choice but to attack some land-based facilities... After we dropped our bombs I thought the city of Darwin was blown away.

To one of the *Soryu*'s Zeke pilots, Kaname Harada, the Darwin raid was one of the easiest missions he flew. "We got information that there was a number of freighters entering Darwin ... we were there to protect our bombers in anticipation that there would be Australian fighters attacking," he recalled. "But there was nothing." As top cover for the raid the *Soryu*'s fighters were in a position to watch proceedings as the raid unfolded. Harada watched as what is considered to have been the USS *Peary* was attacked, recalling that "It was a dive-bomb attack from 5000m and the plume of smoke went 200m up in the air ... a bomb I saw I dropped hit the heart of the vessel, [and I saw] the first spark and then the next moment the vessel disappeared."

A Kate Pilot, Haruo Yoshino, recalled, "19 February 1942 our *Kaga* attack unit delivered a sudden attack on Port Darwin... The Type 97s attacked a government office district and merchant ships in the port, and the Type 99s damaged an airfield, hangars and merchant ships." Another Kate pilot, Taisuke Maruyama from the *Hiryu*, related, "my Type 97 ... was armed with an 800 kilogram land-based bomb. For this mission we did level bombing. Antiaircraft shells exploded near our formation, and it caused my airplane to swerve up and down, and also left to right. Still, our bombing was successful, and every airplane returned safely to our carrier."

Of the 188 Japanese aircraft involved in the initial raid, seven losses were admitted to by the attack leader, Mitsuo Fuchida. However, only two Japanese aircraft have been confirmed as lost as a result of action over Darwin that day, while a further Val and a Zeke ditched on return to the carriers.

From the claims made and subsequent investigations the losses were incurred as a result of ground fire excluding the two claimed by Oestreicher – since disproved through reference to Allied and Japanese documents, interviews and research, including Oestreicher's own reports. Both were P-40s and both

Although assigned top cover during the raid, fighter pilot FPO1c Kaname Harada from the carrier *Soryu* watched the destruction of the USS *Peary* by Val dive-bombers.

were the result of erroneous reporting by ground observers. The antiaircraft gunners of 14 HAA Battery at the Oval and other sites at Fannie Bay and McMillans, 2 HAA Battery at Berrimah and numerous machine guns and small arms all put up such intense fire that many Val dive-bombers were reported as wavering in their attacks, and while one was reportedly hit by a 3.7-inch round from the Oval battery and crashed into the harbour, there is nothing to substantiate the loss.

Flight Chief Petty Officer Katsuyoshi Tsuru and fellow Val crewmen aboard the *Kaga* during 1941. Tsuru and his pilot, Flyer 1c Takezo Uchikado were killed in the crash of Val No. 3304. (Tsuru family via Bob Piper)

What can be substantiated however is that, far from sacrificing themselves as "self-destruction" as described in the Japanese documentation, the two confirmed losses that day were caused by small-arms fire from a number of sites in the vicinity of the RAAF Station. The first was Val No. 3304, tail number AII-254 from the *Kaga*. The crew comprising 3rd *Shotai* leader and aircraft commander, FCPO Katsuyoshi Tsuru and his pilot, Flyer1c Takezo Uchikado, were killed when their aircraft crashed at Ironstone Knob after being hit by ground fire from the Winnellie Camp on the eastern outskirts of Darwin. Both were buried in a grave adjacent to the crash site and, following investigations, two Australian soldiers, Lance Corporal Fred Terrone and Sapper Dick Spedding, were credited with the downing of the aircraft and commended for their actions.

The second Japanese loss was Zeke No. 5349 from the carrier *Hiryu*, flown by PO1c Hajime Toyoshima. A July 1941 graduate of the 56th Class Oita *Kokutai*, Toyoshima had flown CAP during the Pearl Harbor raids and flew in the Wake Island attack. He was elevated to temporary *Buntaicho* for

The usual aircraft of PO1c Tsugio Matsuyama, A6M2 No. 5349 was flown by PO1c Hajime Toyoshima on February 19, 1942. It was the first intact example to fall into Allied hands in the South West Pacific Area. (Alan Beatty via Bob Piper)

the usual aircraft of PO1c Tsugio Matsuyama, tail coded BII-124. Toyoshima was halfway across Melville Island flight when his engine seized and the propeller shaft sheared; the result of a .303-inch projectile holing his oil tank over Darwin. With no other option, Toyoshima force landed wheels up in a grassy valley, hitting his head on the gun sight and suffering cuts to his face. After exiting the aircraft he tried to put as much distance between it and himself.

THE FORCED LANDING ON MELVILLE ISLAND BY PO1C HAJIME TOYOSHIMA (PP. 76–77)

As part of the carrier *Hiryu's* fighter element PO1c Hajime Toyoshima was to intercept any Allied fighters and strafe targets of opportunity during the attack on Darwin. Having flown as top cover over Pearl Harbor he had also flown in the Wake Island attacks. Elevated to the temporary rank of *Buntaicho* – or group leader – for the Darwin raid he was flying the usual aircraft of PO1c Tsugio Matsuyama. During the inward flight six of the *Hiryu's* Zekes had split from the main force to strafe the Bathurst Island mission and airstrip before commencing the strafing attacks on targets over Darwin. Toyoshima was flying in a circuit strafing the RAAF Station when he was hit by small-arms fire over the Parap Camp at Stuart Park. Heading back for the carriers he was over Melville Island when his engine seized and the propeller sheared off. Toyoshima selected a clear area and force landed on near Snake Bay on Melville Island, striking his head on the gunsight and suffering cuts to his face (**1**). After exiting the aircraft, he set off in an attempt to put as much distance between the Zeke (**2**) and himself. After some time he met up with a group of Aboriginal women and children whom he unsuccessfully tried to befriend. Abandoning the Japanese pilot the women alerted a group of young Aboriginal men led by Matthias Ulungura. Lured across Apsley Strait to the Bathurst Island Mission, he was handed over to Sergeant Les Powell of the 23rd Field Company Royal Australian Engineers. Transported south for interrogation via Darwin and Alice Springs, Toyoshima was assigned POW No. PJW11001. Using the alias Tadao Minami (translated as Southern loyalty), he became a leader at the Cowra POW camp and blew the bugle initiating the August 1944 breakout. He died by his own hand the following day August 5, 1944.

Alerted to his predicament, the Japanese launched a floatplane to rescue him. However he failed to appear and was effectively abandoned and classified as "self-destruction." Toyoshima wandered through the bush for some time before stumbling upon a group of Aboriginal women and children who later abandoned him. He was lured across Apsley Strait by a group of young Aboriginal men led by Matthias Ngapiatulawai (Ulungura) and taken prisoner by Sergeant Les Powell of the 23rd Field Company Royal Australian Engineers at the Bathurst Island Mission. Toyoshima was later transported south for interrogation via Darwin and Alice Springs and assigned POW No. PJW11001. Using the alias Tadao Minami (translated as Southern loyalty), Toyoshima became a leader at the Cowra POW camp and blew the bugle initiating the August 1944 breakout. He died by his own hand the following day.

It was during interrogation by Private Joe Da Costa of Australian Army Intelligence, himself part Filipino and educated in Toyoshima's home prefecture, Kobe, that Toyoshima mentioned he had been hit "over the big silver camp." Investigations confirmed his aircraft was hit by small-arms fire from the Parap Camp and specifically Sappers Tom Lamb and Len O'Shea of the 19th Infantry Battalion. José Manuel "Joe" Da Costa was 19 years old when he joined the Australian Army in November 1941. His Japanese education saw his linguistic skills put to good use at Central Bureau in Melbourne. There he interrogated Toyoshima before heading to Darwin and 57 Special Wireless Section, where he intercepted and translated Japanese radio traffic. He later served in a number of Intelligence units and attained the rank of captain.

Hajime Toyoshima, classmates of 56th Class Oita *Kokutai* and family in 1941. Of 19 class members, only Takeshi Sakamoto survived the war. (Takeshi Sakamoto via Bob Piper)

Two other losses were also recorded in the Japanese operations records, the *Kodochosho*, though the crews were rescued. One, a Val from *Soryu* and lead aircraft in the 6th *Shotai*, ditched near a destroyer on its return to the carriers. The crew, comprising pilot Flyer1c Takeshi Yamada and aircraft commander Flyer1c Kinji Funazaki, were both recovered safely. The second was a Zeke from *Kaga* flown by Flyer1c Yoshio Egawa as the 3rd aircraft in the 2nd *Shotai*. Egawa suffered damage to his undercarriage in action over Darwin, reportedly as a result of hitting a tree, and elected to ditch near a destroyer on his return to the fleet. He too was successfully recovered.

However, the possibility of a third aircraft, a Kate, being lost on return to the carriers remains. Following a recent 2013 translation of the *Kodochosho*, a tabular section on the "Carrier-based attack plane unit – 27 Type 97 attack planes" records: "1035 [hrs Tokyo time] 1C 3/2D [The 3rd plane of the second Flight, 1st Squadron] suffered to the left wheel due to a gunshot and was unable to put out the wheels. It crash-landed on the sea near a friendly destroyer. The crew were rescued by [the destroyer] *Tanikaze*."

Thus, the total losses suffered by the Japanese that day were four aircraft (and possibly a fifth) and two aircrew killed, while PO1c Hajime Toyoshima was captured; a small price to pay for the destruction Fuchida's attacking force had wrought.

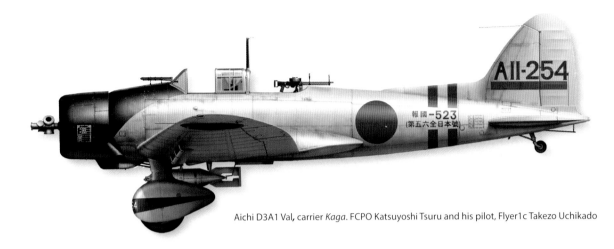

Aichi D3A1 Val, carrier *Kaga*. FCPO Katsuyoshi Tsuru and his pilot, Flyer1c Takezo Uchikado

ALLIED LOSSES

By comparison, the loss of Allied aircraft was disastrous; 27 aircraft were destroyed either in aerial combat or by bombing and strafing on the RAAF Station at Parap Civil 'Drome, on the harbor and on the Tiwi Islands. Those at the RAAF Station fared worst in its perceived importance as a staging base for aircraft heading for the NEI and the ill-fated ABDACOM campaign on Java.

In all 12 aircraft were lost at the RAAF Station during the raids:

Six RAAF Hudson bombers including A16-6, A16-78 and A16-135 of No. 2 Squadron, destroyed by either bombing or strafing; A16-135 was in the No. 13 Squadron hangar. A16-57, also of No. 2 Squadron, was categorized as badly damaged and was written off on March 1, 1942, while No. 13 Squadron lost both A16-72 and A16-141;

Thought to be A16-72 of No. 13 Squadron, this Hudson was parked opposite the 13 Squadron hangar when it was strafed and burnt. It was one of six Hudsons destroyed. (A.H. McEgan via David Vincent)

Two USAAF Curtiss P-40E Warhawks. These "hangar queens" were in the No. 12 Squadron hangar undergoing servicing and repairs when 250kg bombs struck the hangar. One, Serial No. 41-5334, tail number 3, previously thought to have been left by Lt. Joe Kruzel of the 17th Pursuit Squadron (Provisional) following a landing accident on January 26, 1942, was Maj. Pell's aircraft. The other, tail number 29, is suspected to have been Bob McMahon's original Serial No. 41-5421, though this has yet to be confirmed;

One P-40E, tail number "46" of the 33rd Pursuit Squadron (Provisional) USAAF. Lt. William Walker was badly wounded in the left shoulder in the first attack but landed safely at the RAAF Station and was rescued. His aircraft was strafed and destroyed on the tarmac as Lt. Robert H. Vaught prepared to take it into combat.

Consolidated LB-30 Liberator AL521, 7th Bombardment Group. Lts C. B. Kelsay and J. L. Laubscher

Two Beechcraft 18 aircraft, USAAF, Serial Nos. 41-264 and 41-432, destroyed by strafing. These aircraft are thought to have been among a number that evacuated personnel from the Philippines in late 1941 and were impressed into USAAF service, though little is known of their origins, units or previous histories;

One Douglas A-24 of the 91st Bombardment Squadron, 27th Bombardment Group (Light) USAAF, Serial No. 41-15794. The aircraft's wings were removed and the aircraft towed to the RAAF Station for repairs following a landing accident at the Civil 'Drome on February 16. The crew of Lts. J.W. Jacobs and A. Tobias escaped with minor injuries; Tobias with cuts and Jacobs with concussion. The aircraft had completed a dusk supply drop to Lt. Richard Suehr of the 33rd Pursuit Squadron (Provisional) who had force landed near the Marrakai Track south of Darwin. The aircraft was destroyed in the No. 12 Squadron hangar, while a RAAF Wirraway, A20-180 was badly damaged; and one Consolidated LB-30 bomber, AL521, of the 7th Bombardment Group USAAF. Flown by Lieutenants C.B. Kelsay and J.L. Laubscher, the aircraft was transporting Brig. Gen. Patrick J. Hurley from Java to HQ USAFIA in Melbourne and arrived in Darwin on February 18. The aircraft was caught on the ground and strafed and burnt, killing the flight engineer, Staff Sergeant Hugh M. McTavish and wounding the mid-upper gunner, Sergeant Glen L. Beck. Only the wings and engines remained recognizable when Hurley and his aide-de-camp, Lt. Bobb B. Glenn, arrived at the RAAF Station following the raids.

The 12 Squadron hangar showing the tail of Wirraway A20-180, A-24 41-15794, P-40 tail number "29" originally assigned to Lt. McMahon and what is believed to be Maj. Pell's tail number "3." (A.H. McEgan via David Vincent)

Further afield and in aerial combat another 15 aircraft were accounted for as follows:

Eight Curtiss P-40E Warhawks of the 33rd Pursuit Squadron (Provisional) USAAF, lost as a result of aerial combat:

Tail No. 28. Maj. Floyd J. Pell, CO. Killed In Action (KIA)
Tail No. 9. Lt. Max R. Wiecks
Tail No. 22. Lt. Robert F. McMahon
Tail No. 31. Lt. Burt H. Rice
Tail No. 36. Serial No. 41-5456. Lt. John G. Glover
Tail No. 51. Lt. Elton S. Perry. KIA
Tail No. 94. Lt. Charles W. Hughes. KIA
Tail No. 189. Serial No. 41-5368. Lt. Jack R. Peres. KIA

Two Consolidated PBY-4 and one PBY-5 Catalina flying boats of Squadron VP 22 of the US Navy's PatWing 10. Aircraft Bu No. 1214 coded 22-P-4 (previously 102-P-12), Bu No. 1233 coded 22-P-8 and 22-P-41 were at their moorings on Darwin harbor when they were strafed and burnt, though 22-P-41 remained afloat for some time before sinking. Three mechanics working on the aircraft survived the attacks and were rescued by a whaleboat from the seaplane tender USS *William B. Preston*. Aircraft 22-P-41 was an ex-Royal Netherlands Naval Air Service (*Marineluchtvaartdienst* – MLD) PBY-5 model coded Y-41 taken on by PatWing 10 in January 1942 and thus not assigned a Bu No.;

One de Havilland Puss Moth, VH-UPN, belonging to local Northern Territory identity, Roy Edwards, was strafed and burnt at the Parap Civil 'Drome. The aircraft was struck off the Register the following day and Edwards later made a claim for £700 for the aircraft;

One Consolidated PBY-5 Catalina, Bu No. 2306, 22-P-9 (renumbered from 22-P-4) of VP22 PatWing 10 downed off the northwestern tip of Bathurst Island. Flown by Lt. Thomas H. Moorer and Ensign Walter H. Mosley, the aircraft was intercepted by Zekes from the carrier *Kaga* and attacked and downed by PO1c Yoshikazu Nagahama; and One Douglas C-53 transport, No. 41-20051, of the 21st Transport Squadron, USAAF. The aircraft landed at the Bathurst Island Mission airstrip on February 4, 1942 when Darwin was closed in. A wing and aileron were damaged in the process and the aircraft sat at the Mission airstrip awaiting repairs but was strafed and burnt by attacking Zekes from the carrier *Hiryu*.

The wreckage of Consolidated LB-30 AL521 and a P-40 engine outside the 13 Squadron hangar. Brigadier-General Hurley's aide, Lt. Bobb Glenn, described it as "… four smoking engines laying on the ground with a twisted mass of framework strewn around behind them." (John Battaglia Collection NT Library)

Japanese claims for the day were close to post-raid assessments by Australian and American authorities. In all, the claims were detailed in the Japanese records as one PBY and ten P-40s destroyed in the air and five on the ground – two large and three smaller aircraft. A further ten were noted in the Japanese records as, "four large planes, three small planes, three seaplanes" destroyed by strafing, a total of "26 planes (which were all the planes there.)"

On land the claims included hangars at the Civil 'Drome and RAAF Station set on fire, whilst

Naval HQ, the township and main jetty were bombed and set on fire. On the harbor eight ships, two destroyers and a sub-chaser were claimed as being sunk, with a destroyer seriously damaged. "Besides these ships there were a hospital ship and some other small ships but we did not attack them. No air[craft] carriers and [sic] submarines were found in the bay."

In his summary of the various *Kodochosho*, *The Japanese Navy's air-raid against Australia during the World War Two*, Teruaki Kawano provides a more detailed summary, recording that on *Akagi* the pilots and crews reported downing four fighters in combat and destroying four bombers by strafing while destroying two merchant vessels and damaging three others, along with the destruction of a destroyer and the main jetty. Those on the *Kaga* claimed they downed four aircraft while destroying a further five on the ground, destroying hangars and buildings in the township, the RAAF Station and the Civil 'Drome. On the harbor two merchant vessels were claimed as destroyed.

The *Soryu* flyers claimed the sinking of a destroyer, the destruction of an oil tank and military barracks and three merchant vessels damaged whilst the *Hiryu* aircrews claimed the destruction of a cargo vessel and a tanker, with a light cruiser and two merchant vessels damaged. One fighter was claimed as destroyed in the air; a further 12 claimed as destroyed on the ground completed the tally.

The results of the raid were reported as being beyond expectations, however VAdm. Nagumo was reportedly ready to mount a second strike, in contrast to and as if to atone for, his actions at Pearl Harbor where he withdrew – much to Adm. Yamamoto's displeasure. Fuchida, fully aware of the results of the raid and no doubt in expectation of further devastation by the land-based bombers, declared that there was no need. It would be like "snatching a fan from a geisha" he countered. Any thoughts of a second strike were dismissed.

Fuchida later commented that the raid "Seemed hardly worthy of us. If ever a sledgehammer was used to crack an egg it was then." He later wrote:

> [The] job to be done was hardly worthy of the Nagumo Force. The harbor, it is true, was crowded with all kinds of ships, but a single pier and a few waterfront buildings appeared to be the only port installations. The airfield on the outskirts of the town, though

The de Havilland Puss Moth of local personality, Roy Edwards, lies in ruins at the Darwin Civil 'Drome following the raid.

Ray Jackson (right) and fellow RAAF Bomb Disposal Unit, "Lofty," with an unexploded 250kg bomb, one of a number found on the RAAF Station following the raids. (Ray Jackson)

fairly large, had no more than two or three small hangars, and in all there were only twenty-odd planes of various types scattered about the field. No planes were in the air. A few attempted to take off as we came over but were quickly shot down, and the rest were destroyed where they stood. Antiaircraft fire was intense but largely ineffectual, and we quickly accomplished our objectives.

A total of 82,050kg of bombs were dropped by the Kates and Vals in the morning attack while a further 32,050kg were dropped by the Bettys and Nells in the noon raid, an overall total of 114,100kg.

Japanese pilot Kaname Harada described USS *Peary*'s loss when "a bomb… hit the heart of the vessel, [and I saw] the first spark and then the next moment the vessel disappeared." Eighty-eight US Navy personnel died with the ship.

As the Japanese bombers flew back to their bases and the *Kido Butai* headed for Staring Bay the Darwin defenders counted the cost of the attacks. In all 27 Allied aircraft were destroyed, the township and airfields shattered, shipping sunk, at least 236 persons killed and a further 300 injured. Of 67 ships in the harbour, ranging from the private launch *Sea Dog* to the 12,568-ton United States Army Transport (USAT) *Meigs*, six major vessels including the USS *Peary* were sunk in the harbour and two off the Tiwi Islands while a lugger, two launches and a coal hulk were also sunk. Fifteen vessels were damaged, four with only minor damage, while 20 escaped unscathed. Despite Japanese claims, *Manunda* was badly damaged by Val dive-bombers, with 12 deaths and many wounded reported.

A post-attack photo of the harbor taken by a Japanese C5M2 Babs of 3 *Kokutai* at 1010hrs Tokyo time. The oil tanks are at upper left while the *British Motorist* burns at centre.

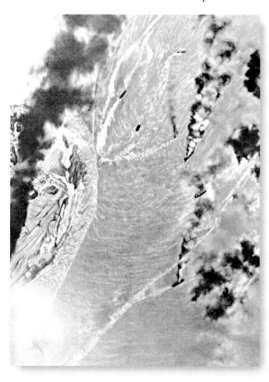

In the town itself the damage was considerable, caused in the main by the 800kg bombs dropped by the Kates. At least six landed in the wharf area hitting the vessel *Neptuna* and cutting the T-shaped jetty, killing 23 waterside workers, or "wharfies." From the wharf area they detonated along the Esplanade and Mitchell Street, destroying a number of government buildings and residences including the post office where ten persons died. One landed near Government House but failed to detonate while others landed in the harbor. A further six landed near the Kahlin Hospital, possibly targeted as Larrakeyah Barracks and causing severe damage.

And through it all the Qantas Short S23 flying boat, *Camilla*, rode at her moorings below Stokes Hill, obscured by smoke drifting across from oil fires and the stricken vessel *Neptuna*. With the raid over, Qantas pilots Bill Crowther and Bert Hussey rushed to the flying boat base and after a quick inspection and some minor repairs they took off as *Neptuna*, her holds full of ammunition, blew up, scattering

Port Darwin – Carrier strike

Aircraft	No. launched	Aborts	Total attacking	Ordnance load	Ordnance released	Tonnage (kgs)
B5N2 Kates	81	Nil	81	One x 800kg bomb	81 x 800kg	64,800kg
D3A1 Vals	71	Nil	71 – one lost after release, MN3304	One x 250kg bomb	69 (2 x hang-ups – Vals returned with bombs)	17,250kg
A6M2 Zekes	36	Nil	36	Nil	Nil	Nil
Totals	188	Nil	188	152 bombs	150 bombs	82,050kg

Port Darwin – Land-based strike

Aircraft	No. launched	Aborts	Total attacking	Ordnance load	Ordnance released	Tonnage (kgs)
G4M1 Bettys	27	Nil	27	212 x 60kg and one x 250kg	212 x 60kg and one x 250kg	12,970kg
G3M2 Nells	27	Nil	27	318 x 60 kg	318 x 60 kg	19,080kg
Totals	54	Nil	54	531 bombs	531 bombs	32,050kg

Totals

Total No. bombs: 681
Total tonnage both carrier and land-based attacks (kgs): 114,100kg

wreckage hundreds of yards. *Camilla* made it safely to Groote Eylandt that evening.

At the Civil 'Drome, bombs and strafing severely damaged the Qantas/ Guinea Airways hangar, vehicles and buildings, including an ammunition store while the Puss Moth of local Roy Edwards was destroyed on the tarmac. At the RAAF Station, the damage from the first raid was being assessed when the 54 land-based bombers appeared. Both raids left the facility severely damaged. A preliminary assessment sent by telegram to ABDACOM and headquarters in Melbourne that evening read "number 12 and 13 squad hangar totally destroyed. Station store extensively damaged… Officer's mess airmen's quarters workshop and transport shed damaged, southern wing hospital destroyed casualties not repetition not completely assessed. Damage to runway (a) north west 3 bombs one unexploded. Serviceable (b) north reserve 7 craters unserviceable 12 hours. Further follow." The base was operational the following day.

The deaths at the RAAF Station numbered eight and while the total number might never be known, the 236 deaths thus far confirmed by a number of researchers and the Northern Territory Library's *Roll of Honour*, were as follows:

LEFT
An American serviceman surveys bomb damage to the 1884 Courthouse and Police Station, which was taken over by the Navy as HMAS *Melville*.

RIGHT
A near miss by an 800kg bomb left a large crater to the right of the Darwin Cenotaph. Damage to the Administrator's Residence (Government House) is visible at rear.

Virtually nothing remained of the *Neptuna* after she blew up at the main jetty. The coastal trader *Barossa* was trapped at the inner berth and badly damaged though she was later repaired.

Nationality	Civilian	Navy	Army	Air Force	Total
Australian	39 incl. 23 waterside workers	7	2	7	55
	Unknown aboard Australian hospital ship *Manunda*				12
American		103	5	5	113
Other	56 mixed nationalities including merchant seamen				56
TOTAL					236

Despite the damage and misreported desertions by RAAF personnel, life at the RAAF Station resumed soon after the raids. An airman attends to the daily washing under the badly damaged Officers' Mess. (A.H. McEgan via David Vincent)

AN END AND A BEGINNING

With Darwin reportedly incapacitated as an Allied base for the foreseeable future, the invasion of Bali completed and the plans for invading Timor unhindered, the *Kido Butai* departed and proceeded to Staring Bay for replenishment, any necessary repairs and the replacement of losses.

With the carriers *Shokaku* and *Zuikaku* having rejoined the fleet, Nagumo's force then ranged out over the Pacific before sortieing into the Indian Ocean in late March to conduct attacks on the British fleet, along with attacks on Ceylon, between March 31 and April 10. The following month the battle of the Coral Sea was fought entirely in the air, before the fleet returned to Japan, where it prepared for the planned attack on Midway, named Operation *MI*.

Before the Midway invasion commenced, however, the cracking of the Japanese JN-25b code by

American cryptographers, poor reconnaissance and tactical errors by Nagumo saw the *Kido Butai* attacked by carrier-borne US Navy dive-bombers on June 4. Three carriers, *Akagi*, *Kaga* and *Soryu*, were destroyed as aircraft were being prepared to launch attacks against American carriers. The *Hiryu* survived and managed to get aircraft away for a crippling attack on the carrier *Yorktown* but was later sunk and with it went the hopes of Adm. Isoroku Yamamoto in defeating the Allies. From the defeat at Midway the Japanese were on the back foot and never recovered.

As a result of their actions on February 19, 1942, the American pilots of the 33rd Pursuit Squadron (Provisional) were each awarded the American Distinguished Service Cross, second only to the Medal of Honor, and all but the four killed that day went on to other units in the Pacific and European Theaters. Any acknowledgment by Australia of their actions was less forthcoming however.

In his report as Royal Commissioner to investigate and report on the circumstances of the raids of February 19, Justice Charles Lowe of the Victorian Supreme Court gave them scant credit for their actions, all but dismissing them in stating, "the American P.40's [sic] which were grounded attempted to take off and to attack the Japanese planes. They were, without exception, shot down."

In *The Canberra Times* of February 19, 1992, Australian journalist Frank Cranston also wrote of the raids and, in relating John Glover's death in 1990, remarked that he [Glover] remained "unthanked by Australia for his efforts on our behalf." The same could be said not only of the ten pilots who flew that day but also of all those who stood their ground and fought against the Japanese attacks.

It had taken the Japanese fighters just 30 minutes to decimate the 33rd Pursuit Squadron (Provisional) and in all just over two hours over the two attacks to incapacitate Darwin as a forward base for the Allies and as a foil to the planned invasion of Timor the following day. Less than a month later, however, Darwin and its defences were capable of hitting back with RAAF Hudsons of Nos. 2 and 13 Squadrons while its aerial defences once again hinged on the inexperience of young USAAF pilots, this time those of the 49th Pursuit Group as the RAAF reequipped.

Glad that's over! A gun crew aboard HMAS *Platypus* takes a break following the first raid. (Gordon McAndrew via Roger Smith)

DARWIN TODAY

Having survived Japanese raids from February 19, 1942 to November 12, 1943 and the destructive forces of Cyclone Tracy on December 24, 1974, which left the city all but destroyed, Darwin today is a vibrant cosmopolitan capital belying its former reputation as a "cowboy town." While Darwin remains a vital part of Australia's military presence in the north, it is also a repository for its wartime heritage. Reminders of the military build-up from the 1920s to war's end and beyond remain, as does the occasional find of an unexploded Japanese bomb.

The major sites and relics associated with the attacks on Darwin are many and some of the more significant in terms of the February 19, 1942 attacks remain in and around the city:

Naval oil tanks
Now a part of the Naval Oil Fuel Installation (OFI), the original storage tanks commenced in 1924 remain. Despite being bombed during the war years, they remain operational and are an integral and visible part of Darwin's wartime history. As an operational naval facility the OFI is not normally accessible to the public.

Darwin's Wharf
The first bombs fell on the wharf, killing 23 waterside workers, and while the old jetty has long since been replaced, those killed are commemorated near the entrance to the wharf precinct. A brief remembrance ceremony is conducted there each February 19.

Image of Darwin's stately
Government House.
(Pauleen Cass)

The Darwin Cenotaph.
(Darwin City Council)

Government House

Darwin's first official residence, the House of Seven Gables as it is known, has been the home of the Government Administrator since the 1880s. An 800kg bomb demolished the Administrator's offices in the first raid, killing a young housemaid, Daisy Martin. Government House is open to the public on designated occasions.

Darwin Cenotaph

First erected opposite Government House in 1921, the Cenotaph now stands on the site of the wartime 3.7-inch antiaircraft battery. The memorial was near-missed by an 800kg bomb on February 19, 1942 and now hosts large crowds at the commemorative events of the February 19, 1942 attacks and ANZAC Day each April 25.

USS *Peary* gun. (Pauleen Cass)

Buel plaque. (Pauleen Cass)

The Esplanade – USS *Peary* gun and Buel memorial

In a quiet corner of Darwin's Esplanade, two events associated with the American involvement in Darwin's defence are commemorated each February 19. Overlooking the wreck of the USS *Peary*, her forward gun commemorates the 88 seamen who lost their lives. Adjacent is a plaque commemorating the actions of Lt. Robert J. Buel, the first casualty of the air war over northern Australia.

Larrakeyah Barracks

The site of the Australian Military's Northern Command, Larrakeyah Barracks retains a number of its prewar art deco style buildings including the sergeants' and officers' messes, and headquarters building, along with wartime defence strongpoints and gun emplacements. Designated as a target on February 19, 1942, six 800kg bombs landed close to the nearby Kahlin Hospital, since demolished. As an operational base, public access to Larrakeyah Barracks is not normally permitted.

Fannie Bay AA site

Located near the entry to East Point Reserve, the four gun mounts and command bunker of the AA battery site have been conserved for public access and are protected under the NT Heritage Conservation Act. During the Japanese raids of February 19, 1942, its 3.7-inch guns fired some 80 rounds.

East Point fortifications and Port War

Now a public reserve, East Point (Port War) is a large precinct of prewar and wartime sites including 6-inch gun positions, 9.2-inch gun emplacements, ammunition stores, artificers' workshops, control rooms, observation

Fannie Bay AA site command post.

This scarred Australian flag flew over the RAAF Station through the Japanese attacks. (Norman Cramp, Darwin Military Museum)

strongpoints and the anti-submarine boom anchor point. The Royal Australian Artillery Association runs a museum facility, which incorporates the Darwin Defence Experience providing information and displays on the Japanese attacks and Darwin's role in World War II.

Darwin Civil 'Drome – Qantas/Guinea Airways hangar and Ross Smith Avenue

The only reminder of what was the "Northern Gateway" to Australia for famous aviators of the 1920s and '30s, is the former 1934 Qantas hangar. Severely damaged in the first Japanese attack, the hangar is now a museum facility and bears the marks of Japanese strafing in its framework. The former Civil 'Drome's main runway is now Ross Smith Avenue, a major thoroughfare in suburban Parap.

Toyoshima's Zeke.

Fujita diver. (Geoff and Lois Helyar Collection, NT Library)

RAAF station

A part of the RAAF's strategic presence in the north, the RAAF base has retained many of its original buildings while accommodating modern facilities. The officer commanding's residence, officers', sergeants' and old airmen's messes, headquarters, transport section, No. 13 Squadron workshops, airmen's quarters, and recreation building, most of which were severely damaged in the Japanese attacks, were restored and remain in use. As an operational base, public access is not normally permitted.

PO1c Hajime Toyoshima's A6M2 Zeke and related artifacts

Hajime Toyoshima's aircraft deteriorated over many years until it was handed to the Aviation Historical Society of the Northern Territory (AHSNT) by the Milikapiti community. It is now displayed at Darwin's aviation museum facility, along with associated artifact material. Other displays include the tailplane of Lt. Peres' P-40, the engine of Lt. Walker's P-40, a porthole cover from *Don Isidro* and bullet-scarred girders from the 12 Squadron hangar.

Crosses and a font

Perhaps the most unusual reminder of the initial Japanese attacks on Darwin came from the Japanese themselves. In 1959 the Fujita Salvage Company commenced salvaging a number of the wartime wrecks in Darwin harbour and over two years the Japanese formed a close relationship with the people of Darwin. As a mark of respect, they produced 70 crosses and a baptismal font from salvaged brass and presented them to Darwin's Uniting Church.

BIBLIOGRAPHY

Published sources
Alford, Bob, *Japanese Air Forces Over the NWA 1942–1945* (Thailand, self-published, 2011)
Alford, Bob, *Darwin's Air War* (Aviation Historical Society of the Northern Territory, Revised Edition, 2010)
Bartsch, William H., *Every Day a Nightmare. American Pursuit Pilots in the Defense of Java, 1941–1942* (Texas A&M University Press, 2010)
Darwin Military Museum, *Through Japanese Eyes – The First Attacks on Darwin Narrated.* Translations by Haruki, Yoshida with notes by Lewis, Dr. Tom, OAM and Williams, Dr. Peter (Darwin, 2010)
Edmonds, Walter D., *They Fought With What They Had* (Little, Brown and Company, 1951)
Gillison, Douglas, *Royal Australian Air Force 1939–42* (Australian War Memorial, 1962)
Griffith, Owen, *Darwin Drama* (Bloxhall and Chambers, 1946)
Lewis, Dr. Tom and Ingman, Peter, *Carrier Attack. The Complete Guide to Australia's own Pearl Harbor* (Avonmore Books, 2013)
Lockwood, Douglas, *Australia's Pearl Harbour* (Cassell Australia, 1966)
Lowe, Justice Charles, *Commission of Inquiry Concerning the Circumstances Connected With the Attack Made by Japanese Aircraft at Darwin on 19th February, 1942. Reports by Commissioner (Mr. Justice Lowe), Together With Observations Thereon by the Departments of the Navy, Army, Air and Interior* (Commonwealth Government Printer. Presented by Command, October 5, 1945)
Messimer, Dwight R., *In the Hands of Fate* (Naval Institute Press, 1985)
Mulholland, Jack, *Darwin Bombed. The Unit History of 14 Heavy Anti-Aircraft Battery* (Australian Military History Publications, 1999)
Piper, Robert, *The Hidden Chapters* (Pagemasters, Australia, 1995)
Powell, Alan, *The Shadow's Edge* (Melbourne University Press, 1988)
Rayner, Robert, *The Army and the Defence of Darwin Fortress* (Rudder Press, 1995)
Rorrison, James D. *Nor the years Contemn: Air War on the Australian Front 1941 – 42.* (Palomar, 1992)
Tagaya, Osamu, *Mitsubishi Type 1* Rikko 'Betty' *Units of World War 2* (Osprey Publishing Ltd, 2001)
Tagaya, Osamu, *Aichi 99 Kanbaku 'Val' Units 1937–42* (Osprey Publishing Ltd, 2012)
Werneth, Ron, *Beyond Pearl Harbor. The Untold Stories of Japan's Naval Airmen* (Schiffer, 2008)

Unpublished manuscripts, reports and research papers
Cisneros, Rafael, Master to Colonel Johnson 3rd Base U.S.A.F.I.A., *Report of Bombing and Sinking of U.S.A.T. 'Don Isidro'* (Brisbane, February 21, 1942)
Kawano, Captain Teruaki, *The Japanese Navy's Air-Raid Against Australia During the World War Two* (Military History Department of the National Institute for Defence Studies. August 29, 1997)
Kiep, Ed De, *Aichi D3A1 Houkoku Inscription* (Research Paper, 2010)

Journals, newspapers, newsletters and magazines
Bullard, Steve, "Were more bombs dropped on Darwin than on Pearl Harbor?" in *Wartime* magazine (Australian War Memorial. No. 59. Winter 2012)

Cranston, Frank, "Ten Men Alone" in *The Canberra Times* (Wednesday, Feb 19, 1992)
Franklin, Matthew, "Bomber asks us to forgive him" in *Sunday Territorian* (February 9, 1992)
Franklin, Matthew, "Japanese flyer recalls bombing raids on Darwin and Pearl Harbor" in
        Northern Territory News (Saturday, December 7, 1991)
Osborne, Tom, "The morning I bombed Darwin" in *Sunday Age* (February 16, 1992 and
        reproduced in the 18 NEI Squadron Association newsletter No. 38. July 1992)

Archives and repositories
Australian War Memorial
MacArthur Memorial Archives, USA. Robert G. Oestreicher file
National Archives of Australia
RAAF Historical Section

Diaries, logbooks and correspondence
Birkett, Gordon. Various items of email correspondence
Ingman, Peter. Various items of email correspondence
Johnston, Shane. Various items of email correspondence
Kitazawa, Noritaka. Military History Dept. National Institute for Defence Studies.
        Correspondence to Bob Piper, dated November 27, 2000
Lambert, Des. Correspondence relating to Aichi D3A1 Val 3304
Lawson, Murry. Correspondence to the author
Lewis, Dr. Tom, AO. Various items of email correspondence
McMahon, Robert F. Correspondence of October 25, 1973 and July 4, 1990
Piper, Bob, Canberra ACT, dated November 27, 2000, and various items of email
        correspondence
Tinkler, Ken. In correspondence to the author, *TO WHOM IT MAY CONCERN*, 1992

Interviews
McMahon, Robert F. Interview with the author, May 12, 1992 and subsequent
        correspondence
Powell, Alan, *Transcript of Interview with Robert G Oestreicher, 19 February 1982*. For
        Northern Territory Oral History Project, Northern Territory Archives Service,
        Darwin
Roberts, Peter, AIF Gunner East Point, re Japanese raid of February 19, 1942. Interview with
        the author, April 4, 1988

Internet sites
Lansdale, James F., *j-aircraft.com* and Pacific Air War History Associates
Millman, Nick, *aviationofjapan.com*
Taylan, Justin, *pacificwrecks.com*

Private notes and files
Bob Alford files including: Robert G. Oestreicher file, 33rd Pursuit Squadron (Provisional) file,
        notes and historical documentation on the February 19, 1942 Darwin raids, notes
        and documentation on Japanese aircraft and units and personnel involved in the
        raids, and documents and notes held on USAAF activities in the Northern Territory
        and Darwin 1942

INDEX